AA Pub Walks &
Cycle Rides

The Peak District

Walk routes researched and written by Neil Coates, John Gillham,
Moira McCrossan and Hugh Taylor
Cycle routes researched and written by Neil Coates
Series managing editor: David Hancock

Produced by AA Publishing
© Automobile Association Developments Ltd 2005
First published 2005

Published by AA Publishing (a trading name of Automobile Association Developments
Limited, whose registered office is Southwood East, Apollo Rise, Farnborough, Hampshire
GU14 0JW; registered number 1878835).

A02013

ISBN-10: 0-7495-4454-6
ISBN-13: 978-0-7495-4454-6

A CIP catalogue record for this book is available from the British Library.

WORCESTERSHIRE COUNTY COUNCIL		
248		
Bertrams	01.07.05	
914.2511	£9.99	
RE		

The contents of this book are believed correct at the time of printing. Nevertheless, the
publishers cannot be held responsible for any errors or omissions or for changes in the
details given in this book or for the consequences of any reliance on the information it
provides. We have tried to ensure accuracy in this book, but things do change and we
would be grateful if readers would advise us of any inaccuracies they may encounter. This
does not affect your statutory rights.

We have taken all reasonable steps to ensure that the walks and cycle rides are safe and
achievable by people with a realistic level of fitness. However, all outdoor activities involve
a degree of risk and the publishers accept no responsibility for any injuries caused to
readers whilst following these walks and cycle rides. For advice on walking and cycling in
safety, see pages 12 to 15.

Visit AA Publishing's website www.theAA.com/bookshop

Page layouts by pentacorbig, High Wycombe
Colour reproduction by Keene Group, Andover
Printed in Spain by Graficas Estella

AA

Pub Walks & Cycle Rides

The Peak District

Locator map

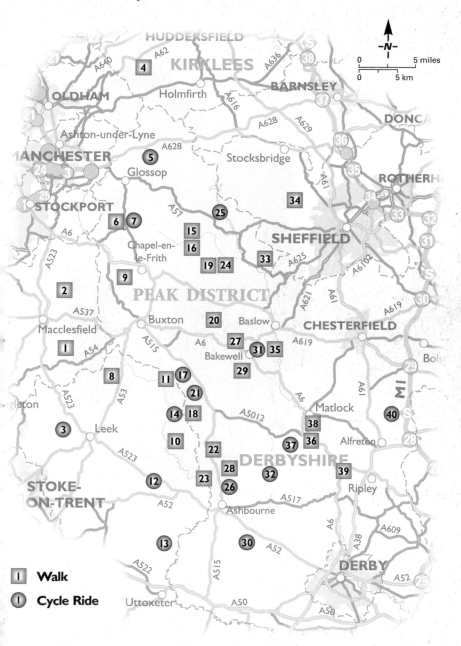

Contents

Picture on page 4: Hope Valley stretching into the distance viewed from Millstone Edge

Contents

The Peak District

The Peak District covers a surprising variety of landscapes, with hills (not too high!), the beautiful River Dove, dales (valleys) and of course, The Peak District National Park. This became the first National Park in Britain, gaining this status in 1951. The park (www.peakdistrict.org) encompasses an impressive 542 square miles (1,404 sq km) of protected land and extends into six counties. The wider parameters of the Peak District have long been a favourite with walkers and ramblers, as part of the 256-mile (412km) long footpath, the Pennine Way National Trail, falls within its boundaries. The region is also easily accessible from several major cities including Manchester, Liverpool and Birmingham, making a day trip a feasible option. Of course, no information on the Peak District would be complete without mentioning Dark Peak or White Peak. Dark Peak is the northern area of moorland and reservoirs with an industrial heritage where the highest points of the area are to be found. White Peak, to the south, is named for the pale limestone which dominates the landscape and is where you'll find the dales (valleys).

The phrase 'up hill and down dale' is particulary appropriate for the Peak District

with many hills (for example Kinder Scout and the Mam Tor ridge) and wildlife-filled dales to explore, from the beauty spot of Dovedale with its much-photographed stepping stones, to Long Dale, Monsal Dale (where you walk across a viaduct), Biggin Dale and the unspoilt Churnet Valley.

This region is also blessed with reservoirs and lakes which make pleasant and easy-to-navigate cycle routes. Cycle rides by water in this book take in Derwent Reservoir, Rudyard Lake, Carsington Water, Combs Reservoir and Dale Dike Reservoir. Similarly easy to negotiate are routes on trackbeds of former railway lines such as the Hayfield to New Mills line, the Churnet Valley line and the Cromford and High Peak Railway. Designated cycle routes include the family-friendly Tissington Trail.

If a pretty village or hamlet is an essential part of your trip then follow the routes that take in Old Glossop, Carsington, Tissington, Ashford-in-the-Water or Osmaston with its thatched cottages and picturesque houses. One walk even takes in the unusually named Flash, England's highest village at 1,518ft (463m).

If you prefer a focus to your day out in the countryside, then follow the walk that takes you past palatial Chatsworth House (www.chatsworth.org), the home of the Duke and Duchess of Devonshire, which has many well-known works of art, a maze and fountains, as well as a restaurant and opportunities for shopping. To delve deeper into England's past, there are routes that go past castles, such as the route along the River Churnet which takes you to Victorian Alton Castle or, not as grand, but just as historic, Peveril Castle in Castleton.

The view from Mam Tor

Using this book

Each walk and cycle ride has a coloured panel giving essential information for the walker and cyclist, including the distance, terrain, nature of the paths, and where to park your car.

1 | **3h00** | **8.5 MILES** | **13.7 KM** | **LEVEL 1** 23 | **4**

SHORTER ALTERNATIVE ROUTE

1h30 | **4 MILES** | **6.4 KM** | **LEVEL 1** 23

2 **MAP:** OS Explorer OL24 White Peak

START/FINISH: Rudyard Old Station, grid ref

3 SJ 955579

TRAILS/TRACKS: old railway trackbed

LANDSCAPE: wooded lake shore, peaceful pastures and meadows

PUBLIC TOILETS: Rudyard village

5 **TOURIST INFORMATION:** Leek, tel 01538 483741

6 **CYCLE HIRE:** none near by

THE PUB: The Abbey Inn, Leek, see Directions to the pub, page 27

7 🛑 Take care along the banks of the lake – keep well away from the shore line

1 **MINIMUM TIME:** The time stated for completing each route is the estimated minimum time that a reasonably fit family group of walkers or cyclists would take to complete the circuit. This does not allow for rest or refreshment stops.

2 **MAPS:** Each route is shown on a detailed map. However, some detail is lost because of the restrictions imposed by scale, so for this reason, we recommend that you use the maps in conjunction with a more detailed Ordnance Survey map. The relevant Ordnance Survey Explorer map appropriate for each walk or cycle is listed.

3 **START/FINISH:** Here we indicate the start location and parking area. There is a six-figure grid reference prefixed by two letters showing which 100km square of the National Grid it refers to. You'll find more information on grid references on most Ordnance Survey maps.

4 **LEVEL OF DIFFICULTY:** The walks and cycle rides have been graded simply (1 to 3) to give an indication of their relative difficulty. Easier routes, such as those with little total ascent, on easy footpaths or level trails, or those covering shorter distances are graded 1. The hardest routes, either

because they include a lot of ascent, greater distances, or are in hilly, more demanding terrains, are graded 3.

5 **TOURIST INFORMATION:** The nearest tourist information office and contact number is given for further local information, in particular opening details for the attractions listed in the 'Where to go from here' section.

6 **CYCLE HIRE:** We list, within reason, the nearest cycle hire shop/centre.

7 🛑 Here we highlight any potential difficulties or dangers along the route. At a glance you will know if the walk is steep or crosses difficult terrain, or if a cycle route is hilly, encounters a main road, or whether a mountain bike is essential for the off-road trails. If a particular route is suitable for older, fitter children we say so here.

About the pub

Generally, all the pubs featured are on the walk or cycle route. Some are close to the start/finish point, others are at the midway point, and occasionally, the recommended pub is a short drive from the start/finish point. We have included a cross-section of pubs, from homely village locals and isolated rural gems to traditional inns and upmarket country pubs which specialise in food. What they all have in common is that they serve food and welcome children.

The description of the pub is intended to convey its history and character and in the 'food' section we list a selection of dishes, which indicate the style of food available. Under 'family facilities', we say if the pub offers a children's menu or smaller portions of adult dishes, and whether the pub has a family room, highchairs, baby-changing facilities, or toys. There is detail on the garden, terrace, and any play area.

DIRECTIONS: If the pub is very close to the start point we state see Getting to the Start. If the pub is on the route the relevant direction/map location number is given, in addition to general directions. In some cases the pub is a short drive away from the finish point, so we give detailed directions to the pub from the end of the route.

PARKING: The number of parking spaces is given. All but a few of the walks and rides start away from the pub. If the pub car park is the parking/start point, then we have been given permission by the landlord to print the fact. You should always let the landlord or a member of staff know that you are using the car park before setting off.

OPEN: If the pub is open all week we state 'daily' and if it's open throughout the day we say 'all day', otherwise we just give the days/sessions the pub is closed.

FOOD: If the pub serves food all week we state 'daily' and if food is served throughout the day we say 'all day', otherwise we just give the days/sessions when food is not served.

BREWERY/COMPANY: This is the name of the brewery to which the pub is tied or the pub company that owns it. 'Free house' means that the pub is independently owned and run.

REAL ALE: We list the regular real ales available on handpump. 'Guest beers' indicates that the pub rotates beers from a number of microbreweries.

DOGS: We say if dogs are allowed in pubs on walk routes and detail any restrictions.

ROOMS: We list the number of bedrooms and how many are en suite. For prices please call the pub.

Please note that pubs change hands frequently and new chefs are employed, so menu details and facilities may change at short notice. Not all the pubs featured in this guide are listed in the *AA Pub Guide*. For information on those that are, including AA-rated accommodation, and for a comprehensive selection of pubs across Britain, please refer to the *AA Pub Guide* or see the AA's website www.theAA.com

Alternative refreshment stops

At a glance you will see if there are other pubs or cafés along the route. If there are no other places on the route, we list the nearest village or town where you can find somewhere else to eat and drink.

☞ Where to go from here

Many of the routes are short and may only take a few hours. You may wish to explore the surrounding area after lunch or before tackling the route, so we have selected a few attractions with children in mind.

Walking and cycling in safety

WALKING

All the walks are suitable for families, but less experienced family groups, especially those with younger children, should try the shorter or easier walks first. Route finding is usually straightforward, but the maps are for guidance only and we recommend that you always take the suggested Ordnance Survey map with you.

Risks

Although each walk has been researched with a view to minimising any risks, no walk in the countryside can be considered to be completely free from risk. Walking in the outdoors will always require a degree of common sense and judgement to ensure that it is as safe as possible, especially for young children.

- Be particularly careful on cliff paths and in upland terrain, where the consequences of a slip can be serious.
- Remember to check tidal conditions before walking on the seashore.
- Some sections of route are by, or cross, busy roads. Remember traffic is a danger even on minor country lanes.
- Be careful around farmyard machinery and livestock.
- Be aware of the consequences of changes in the weather and check the forecast before you set out. Ensure the whole family is properly equipped, wearing warm clothing and a good pair of boots or sturdy walking shoes. Take waterproof clothing with you and carry spare clothing and a torch if you are walking in the winter months. Remember the weather can change quickly at any time of the year, and in moorland and heathland areas, mist and fog can make route finding much harder. In summer, take account of the heat and sun by wearing a hat and carrying enough water.

- On walks away from centres of population you should carry a whistle and survival bag. If you do have an accident requiring emergency services, make a note of your position as accurately as possible and dial 999.

CYCLING

Cycling is a fun activity which children love, and teaching your child to ride a bike, and going on family cycling trips, are rewarding experiences. Not only is cycling a great way to travel, but as a regular form of exercise it can make an invaluable contribution to a child's health and fitness, and increase their confidence and sense of independence.

The growth of motor traffic has made Britain's roads increasingly dangerous and unattractive to cyclists. Cycling with children is an added responsibility and, as with everything, there is a risk when taking them out for a day's cycling. However, in recent years many measures have been taken to address this, including the on-going development of the National Cycle Network (8,000 miles utilising quiet lanes and traffic-free paths) and local designated off-road routes for families, such as converted railway lines, canal towpaths and forest tracks.

In devising the cycle rides in this guide, every effort has been made to use these designated cycle paths, or to link

them with quiet country lanes and waymarked byways and bridleways. Unavoidably, in a few cases, some relatively busy B-roads have been used to link the quieter, more attractive routes.

Rules of the road
- Ride in single file on narrow and busy roads.
- Be alert, look and listen for traffic, especially on narrow lanes and blind bends and be extra careful when descending steep hills, as loose gravel can lead to an accident.
- In wet weather make sure you keep a good distance between you and other riders.
- Make sure you indicate your intentions clearly.
- Brush up on *The Highway Code* before venturing out on to the road.

Off-road safety code of conduct
- Only ride where you know it is legal to do so. It is forbidden to cycle on public footpaths, marked in yellow. The only 'rights of way' open to cyclists are bridleways (blue markers) and unsurfaced tracks, known as byways, which are open to all traffic and waymarked in red.
- Canal towpaths: you need a permit to cycle on some stretches of towpath (www.waterscape.com). Remember that access paths can be steep and slippery and always get off and push your bike under low bridges and by locks.

- Always yield to walkers and horses, giving adequate warning of your approach.
- Don't expect to cycle at high speeds.
- Keep to the main trail to avoid any unnecessary erosion to the area beside the trail and to prevent skidding, especially if it is wet.
- Remember the Country Code.

Cycling with children

Children can use a child seat from the age of eight months, or from the time they can hold themselves upright. There are a number of child seats available which fit on the front or rear of a bike and towable two-seat trailers are worth investigating. 'Trailer bicycles', suitable for five- to ten-year-olds, can be attached to the rear of an adult's bike, so that the adult has control, allowing the child to pedal if he/she wishes. Family cycling can be made easier by using a tandem, as it can carry a child seat and tow trailers. 'Kiddy-cranks' for shorter legs can be fitted to the rear seat tube, enabling either parent to take their child out cycling. With older children it is better to purchase the right size bike rather than one that is too big, as an oversized bike will be difficult to control, and potentially dangerous.

Preparing your bicycle

A basic routine includes checking the wheels for broken spokes or excess play in the bearings, and checking the tyres for punctures, undue wear and the correct tyre pressures. Ensure that the brake blocks are firmly in place and not worn, and that cables are not frayed or too slack. Lubricate hubs, pedals, gear mechanisms and cables. Make sure you have a pump, a bell, a rear rack to carry panniers and, if cycling at night, a set of working lights.

Preparing yourself

Equipping the family with cycling clothing need not be an expensive exercise. Comfort is the key when considering what to wear. Essential items for well-being on a bike are padded cycling shorts, warm stretch leggings (avoid tight-fitting and seamed trousers like jeans or baggy tracksuit trousers that may become caught in the chain), stiff-soled training shoes, and a wind and waterproof jacket. Fingerless gloves will add to your comfort.

A cycling helmet provides essential protection if you fall off your bike, so they are particularly recommended for young children learning to cycle.

Wrap your child up with several layers in colder weather. Make sure you and those with you are easily visible by car drivers and other road users, by wearing light-coloured or luminous clothing in daylight and reflective strips or sashes in failing light and when it is dark.

What to take with you
Invest in a pair of medium-sized panniers (rucksacks are unwieldy and can affect balance) to carry the necessary gear for you and your family for the day. Take extra clothes with you, the amount depending on the season, and always pack a light wind/waterproof jacket. Carry a basic tool kit (tyre levers, adjustable spanner, a small screwdriver, puncture repair kit, a set of Allen keys) and practical spares, such as an inner tube, a universal brake/gear cable, and a selection of nuts and bolts. Also, always take a pump and a strong lock.

Cycling, especially in hilly terrain and off-road, saps energy, so take enough food and drink for your outing. Always carry plenty of water, especially in hot and humid weather conditions. Consume high-energy snacks like cereal bars, cake or fruits, eating little and often to combat feeling weak and tired. Remember that children get thirsty (and hungry) much more quickly than adults so always have food and diluted juices available for them.

And finally, the most important advice of all—enjoy yourselves!

USEFUL CYCLING WEBSITES

NATIONAL CYCLE NETWORK
A comprehensive network of safe and attractive cycle routes throughout the UK.

It is co-ordinated by the route construction charity Sustrans with the support of more than 450 local authorities and partners across Britain.

For maps, leaflets and more information on the designated off-road cycle trails across the country contact

www.sustrans.org.uk

www.nationalcyclenetwork.org.uk

LONDON CYCLING CAMPAIGN
Pressure group that lobbies MPs, organises campaigns and petitions in order to improve cycling conditions in the capital. It provides maps, leaflets and information on cycle routes across London.

www.lcc.org.uk

BRITISH WATERWAYS
For information on towpath cycling, visit

www.waterscape.com

FORESTRY COMMISSION
For information on cycling in Forestry Commission woodland see

www.forestry.gov.uk/recreation

CYCLISTS TOURING CLUB
The largest cycling club in Britain, provides information on cycle touring, and legal and technical matters

www.ctc.org.uk

Rossen Clough

A short circular walk through the hidden valley of Rossen Clough, and back via Croker Hill's well-known radio tower.

Croker Hill and Jodrell Bank

Croker Hill is a well-known sight for miles around, although at 1,318ft (402m) it's not in itself particularly high. The reason for its familiarity is a huge telecommunications tower that sits astride its open summit ridge, like a chunky lighthouse decorated

with satellite dishes and antennae sweeping its gaze over the vast plains of northern Cheshire. The tower is 286ft (87m) high and relays radio and television signals across Cheshire and the North West. The engineers chose the location deliberately, since it represents the last of the Peak's westerly ridges, and beyond it the almost dead flat land extends across to the Mersey Basin and ultimately the Irish Sea. Dotted out on the plain you can make out historic Cheshire salt towns like Northwich and Middlewich, but if the weather is clear you

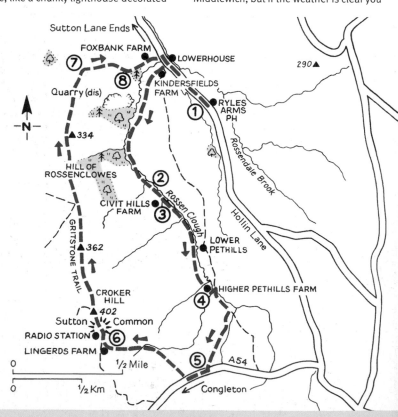

may even be able to see the Shropshire Hills, or the Clywdian Range just over the North Wales border. To the south west lies the bulky spurs of The Cloud, near Congleton, and also Mow Cop, close to Kidsgrove. Looking northwards urban Manchester extends into the murky distance, with the Pennines beyond. Eastwards, and much closer at hand, is the rugged landscape of the Peak District, including the distinctive shapes of Tegg's Nose and Shutlingsloe.

The theme of communications is echoed by another unique man-made feature that is clearly visible, weather permitting, 8 miles (12.9km) west of Croker Hill. The massive white dish of Jodrell Bank's radio telescope peers up at the sky from its movable gantry, as it has done since it clicked into action in 1957. Over the succeeding years the Lovell Telescope, which measures 250ft (76m) in diameter, has been used by both the Americans and the Soviet Union to receive radio waves from deep space.

Looking across to Macclesfield Forest from Croker Hill

MAP: OS Explorer OL24 White Peak
START/FINISH: park at the Ryles Arms (ask permission beforehand), grid ref SJ 938694
PATHS: sloping field paths and tracks, occasionally boggy, 20 stiles and gates
LANDSCAPE: sheltered, part-wooded valley, open grassy ridges
PUBLIC TOILETS: none on route
TOURIST INFORMATION: Macclesfield, tel 01625 504114/5
THE PUB: Ryles Arms, Higher Sutton, see start of route
❶ Some of the paths can be boggy

Getting to the start
From the Arighi Bianchi crossroads on the inner ring road in Macclesfield take the A523 south towards Leek. In 0.5 mile (800m) turn left at the traffic lights on to Byrons Lane, signed for Sutton and Wincle. Go through Sutton Lane Ends and pass the Lamb Inn to find the the Ryles Arms in a further 1.5 miles (2.4km) on the left.

Researched and written by: Neil Coates, Andrew McCloy

the walk

1 From the **Ryles Arms** turn right and walk 500yds (457m) to a narrow, sloping rough lane almost opposite the entrance to **Lowerhouse Farm**. Turn up this lane and continue on past **Kinderfields Farm** with the hilltop communications tower ahead. Ignore occasional turnings on the left, and instead carry on along the wide lane up the secluded valley bottom for almost 0.75 mile (1.2km).

2 After crossing a cattle grid the rising lane approaches **Civit Hills Farm**. Go through the waymarked bridlegate on the left and, dropping down a little, walk across a rough field through scrub towards the far fence, with the farm above (right) and the brook below. This section may be very marshy.

3 Go through a gate and on past a small open pond, then continue along the valley bottom following blue bridleway waymarks through successive gates. Keep the brook on your left and, resisting the urge to cross a footbridge to **Lower Pethills**, veer slightly uphill towards another gate and cross an open field to reach **Higher Pethills Farm**.

4 In the middle of the buildings turn left and walk down the main drive. As you approach the lane at the bottom turn right through a gate. Go straight ahead across a high grassy bank. At a gate, where the bridleway is indicated straight on, turn right for a footpath (yellow arrow) up a short sunken track. After swinging half left walk out across a field beside a line of hawthorn trees and, via fence stiles well left of a barn, cross two more open fields to reach the road at the top.

what to look for

For the second half of the walk you will be following the Gritstone Trail, a 35-mile (56km) route that runs through Cheshire from Kidsgrove in the south to Disley in the north. Croker Hill is one of its highest points. The Gritstone Trail is shown on the ground by yellow waymark discs with a 'G' in a footprint. It makes a stimulating two- or three-day outing, or a series of short circular walks.

5 Turn right and walk along the verge for 160yds (146m), before turning right again on a rough farm track. Now follow the **Gritstone Trail** waymarks for several short field paths up to reach the **telecommunications tower**, making for the top left corner of the final field by **Lingerds Farm**.

6 Turn right and walk along the glorious ridge-top track for almost 1.5 miles (2.4km), ignoring paths off to the left, and passing just to the left of the small summit known as **Hill of Rossenclowes**.

7 The route finally drops down the edge of a field with a row of trees on your right. At the bottom, go right over a stile and down through a sloping field. Keep to the right of the shallow valley, heading towards **Foxbank Farm** below.

8 At the wall at the bottom go through a gate by a plantation on to a grassy path around the right-hand side of the buildings, then drop down steeply to the stile in the bottom corner of the field to return to the lane. Turn right to return to the pub.

Ryles Arms

This very popular comfortable country dining inn extends a warm welcome to ramblers stopping off for refreshment. Built around 260 years ago, the cream-washed and plant-festooned building is named after John Ryles, the first banker in Macclesfield, and was originally a mint. Inside you will find a superbly carved wooden bar fronting a part-flagged, part-tiled drinking area, furnished with comfortable wall benches, leather chairs and large tables. The rest of the pub is open plan and has a mix of furnishings, from old settles and imposing portraits to modern designer tables and chairs. There is a separate dining area with service by uniformed young waitresses.

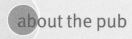

about the pub

Ryles Arms
Hollin Lane
Higher Sutton, Macclesfield
Cheshire SK11 0HN
Tel 01260 252244
www.rylesarms.com

DIRECTIONS: see Getting to the start	
PARKING: 35	
OPEN: daily, all day	
FOOD: daily, all day	
BREWERY/COMPANY: free house	
REAL ALE: Theakston Best, guest beer	
DOGS: no dogs allowed	
ROOMS: 5 en suite	

Food

Food is home-made using locally sourced produce whenever possible. Dishes range from traditional steak and kidney pudding or roast beef and Yorkshire pudding to the more adventurous dishes such as grilled tuna with tomato and coriander sauce, or pork medallions stuffed with red onion and apple chutney with a tomato, shallot and paprika sauce.

Family facilities

Children are welcome in the pub until early evening. In addition to a children's menu smaller portions are available from the main list. There is an extensive rear heated patio with good views.

Alternative refreshment stops

The Lamb at Sutton Lane Ends.

☛ Where to go from here

Hilly Billy Ice Cream is based at Blaze Farm, Wilboarclough, just south east of the walk. Apart from the ice cream, which is made here, there is also a farm trail and the chance to see new-born calves and lambs in season. At Jodrell Bank you can view the Lovell Telescope up close from the observational pathway, and visit the 3-D theatre, arboretum and discovery centre. The Planetarium and some other facilities are closed as part of a 3-year development programme (www.jb.man.ac.uk).

White Nancy above Bollington

Exploring a short but scenic ridge, with a strange landmark, above the leafy town of Bollington.

Kerridge Hill and White Nancy

Bollington lies just outside the far western edge of the Peak District National Park, but it continues to attract walkers and sightseers due in part to the short but inviting ridge of Kerridge Hill that overlooks the small Cheshire town. However, it's not just the superb views that will hold your attention, but also the curiously shaped monument that occupies the far northern tip of the hill.

Visible from below, and for some distance around for that matter, since it stands at 920ft (280m) above sea level, White Nancy is a round stone construction that was built by the local Gaskell family in 1820 to commemorate the Battle of Waterloo. It was originally an open shelter with a stone table and benches, and was presumably a popular spot for picnics, but gradual decay and occasional vandalism led to it being bricked up, and now the building has no discernible door or windows. Nor does it bear any plaque or information panel, and most striking of all it is painted bright white. In terms of shape it resembles a large bell, or perhaps a giant chess pawn, with a large base that tapers into an odd little point. As for its name, the most entertaining version suggests that Nancy was the name of one of the eight horses that pulled the heavy stone table to the summit when the tower was built. Beacons are still lit next to it to mark special occasions.

For all its scenic qualities the lower western slopes of Kerridge Hill are still quarried, although it's not visible on the walk until you reach the main summit ridge. The dressed stone is used for roofing slates and paving slabs and originally it was removed via narrow boats on the Macclesfield Canal which also served the mills and factories that once dotted the Bollington area. For a while, shallow pits in the hill even yielded enough coal to supply the local engine houses, as steam power replaced water power during the Industrial Revolution's relentless advance.

But inevitably your eye will be drawn to sights further afield, and if the weather is clear there will be good views across Macclesfield and the Cheshire Plain to the Mersey Estuary, the urban sprawl of Greater Manchester, as well as the long, high outline of the Pennines away to the north.

Left: Bollington & Clarence Mill
Top right: Distant Rainowlow seen from Kerridge Ridge Path above Waulkmill Wood

the walk

1 Walk up **Church Street**, turn right at the Crown into **Lord Street** and walk to the top of a steep hill. Go left along **Cow Lane**, a cul-de-sac, and through the gate at the far end. Bear half right up a sloping field and aim for the gate and cattle grid at the far left top corner.

2 Turn left on to grass-centred farm track and follow this all the way down to the lane in the bottom of the valley. Turn right, and then almost immediately fork right again past some terraced cottages. A weir and pond below on your left are all that remain of the former silk mill. Follow this path through the Woodland Trust's **Waulkmill Wood**.

3 Leave the wood via a stile and go across the lower part of a sloping field, then in the second aim for the buildings on the far side. Follow the gated path around to the right, and on through successive fields.

2h00	3.5 MILES	5.7 KM	LEVEL 1 2 3

MAP: OS Explorer OL24 White Peak
START/FINISH: kerbside parking on Church Street or Lord Street in Bollington, grid ref SJ 937775
PATHS: easy field paths and farm tracks, about 20 stiles and handgates
LANDSCAPE: mostly gentle rolling pasture and small pockets of woodland
PUBLIC TOILETS: Bollington town centre
TOURIST INFORMATION: Macclesfield, tel 01625 504114/5
THE PUB: Church House Inn, Bollington, near start of route
One short, sharp descent

Getting to the start

From the A625 Macclesfield bypass, take the turn signed for Bollington (B5090, Palmerston Street). Go beneath the high aqueduct and keep left, rising to a mini-roundabout; Church Street is on the right.

Researched and written by: Neil Coates, Andrew McCloy

what to look for

In the mid-1800s there were as many as thirteen mills in Bollington, spinning cotton and silk, and later synthetic fibres such as rayon. The last cotton mill closed in 1960, but as you may see, towards the bottom of Lord Street and elsewhere, some of the town's surviving mill buildings have a new lease of life as modern offices and flats. Another fascinating throwback to a previous industrial age is the impressive Telford-designed aqueduct, which carries the Macclesfield Canal high above the main road through Bollington.

4 Go over a stile with a **Gritstone Trail** waymark (a footprint with the letter 'G') and along the bottom edge of a newly planted broadleaf woodland, then down a walled track through woodland to reach the main road at **Tower Hill**.

5 Turn right and walk along the pavement, past the **Rising Sun Inn**, for 0.5 mile (800m). Turn right into **Lidgetts Lane**, then as it bends almost immediately left/right go over a high stile ahead beside a gate and on to a gated track past a row of hawthorn trees. Swinging left follow this grassy path up to the ridge above – ignore the lower route by the right-hand fence.

6 Follow the obvious hilltop track all the way along the spine of **Kerridge Hill**, ignoring tracks off left and right.

7 After admiring the views at the monument (**White Nancy**) at the far end, drop sharply down the paved, stepped path beyond, with **Bollington** spread out below, then cross a sunken farm lane and continue down beside two more steep fields to reach a stile and steps back into **Cow Lane/Lord Street**. Walk downhill and turn left at the **Crown** to return to the start.

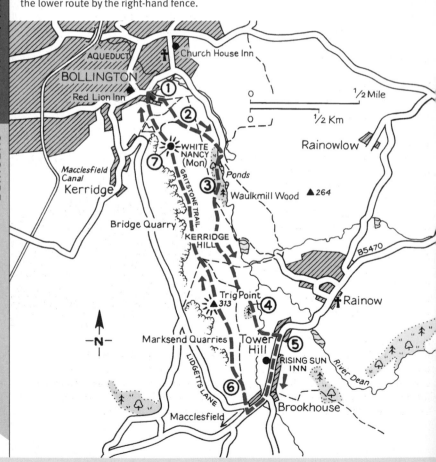

Church House Inn

This quiet corner of Cheshire's largest village is where the discerning drop in for carefully prepared lunchtime snacks and evening meals. Add top-notch beers on hand pump and a cosy and convivial atmosphere, and this genuinely unspoilt street corner local is the place to head to after your walk. Colourful hanging baskets and window boxes add a splash of colour to the stone exterior and etched glass windows in summer. Inside is a jumble of rooms filled with upholstered wall benches, ancient pews and old trestle tables, and warmed in winter by open log fires. The walls are adorned with paintings, local photographs and collections of old brewery jugs. Totally unpretentious – a great all-round pub.

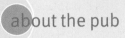

about the pub

Church House Inn
Church Street, Bollington
Cheshire SK10 5PY
Tel 01625 574014

DIRECTIONS: see Getting to the start
PARKING: street parking
OPEN: daily
FOOD: daily
BREWERY/COMPANY: free house
REAL ALE: Black Sheep Bitter, Timothy Taylor's Landlord, Greene King IPA
DOGS: no dogs allowed

Food

Home-made bar food ranges from good pub favourites like steak and ale pie, lasagne and chilli on the printed menu to freshly made soups, pork steak in Stilton and mushroom sauce and Thai vegetable curry on the daily changing blackboard menu.

Family facilities

If you plan to eat at Church House then children are made very welcome and smaller portions are available. Unfortunately the pub has no garden.

Alternative refreshment stops

In Bollington, try the Poacher's Inn, a free house that has a beer garden and allows children inside away from the bar. Along the route is the newly refurbished Rising Sun Inn at Brookhouse.

☛ Where to go from here

Near by in Macclesfield are the Silk Museum (part of the Heritage Centre) and Paradise Mill, both in the town centre (www.silk-macclesfield.org).

Along Rudyard Lake

CYCLE

③

Relive the Edwardian era on this easy route beside picturesque Rudyard Reservoir, source of the water for much of the Midlands' canal network.

Rudyard Lake

You've probably passed over, or cycled beside, many a canal and taken them for granted as part of the scenery. The building of the county's canal system was a massive undertaking, but few people consider just where the water comes from to make them operate. The answer is places like Rudyard Lake. This was created in 1800 as a reservoir to supply water to the Caldon Canal, which served Leek and, more significantly, the Trent and Mersey Canal at Stoke-on-Trent, one of Britain's most important canals.

The Dingle Brook would have taken too long to fill the reservoir (and to keep it topped up) so, in addition to the dam, a feeder channel, or leat, was constructed up in the hills to the east of Rushton Spencer.

This collects water from the River Dane as it rushes down from the high Staffordshire moors and delivers it to Rudyard.

When the North Staffordshire Railway line was built between Leek and Macclesfield during the 1840s, the owners realised the reservoir was a potential leisure resource. They ran special excursion trains and laid out walks in the area. One couple had such pleasant memories of the time they spent here they named their son Rudyard Kipling after the area. Wealthy patrons built eccentric boathouses and chalets along the western shore of the lake, and these can still be seen today.

the ride

1 This is an easy there-and-back route from **Rudyard Old Station**, now the base for the little Rudyard Lake Steam Railway. This narrow gauge line follows the course of the former standard gauge line for 1.5 miles (2.4km) along the lake shore, its miniature steam engines providing endless fascination for visitors of all ages. The route follows the track north through cool woodlands to reach the **Dam Station**. As the name suggests, this is adjacent to the dam holding back **Rudyard Lake.** Make a side detour across the dam to a **visitor centre**, café and toilets – here, too, you'll find rowing boat hire and seasonal launch trips on the lake.

Left: Boathouses at Rudyard Lake
Top: View south down Rudyard Reservoir

Rudyard Lake

STAFFORDSHIRE

24

3h00 | **8.5 MILES** | **13.7 KM** | **LEVEL 1**23

SHORTER ALTERNATIVE ROUTE

1h30 | **4 MILES** | **6.4 KM** | **LEVEL 1**23

MAP: OS Explorer OL24 White Peak

START/FINISH: Rudyard Old Station, grid ref SJ 955579

TRAILS/TRACKS: old railway trackbed

LANDSCAPE: wooded lake shore, peaceful pastures and meadows

PUBLIC TOILETS: Rudyard village

TOURIST INFORMATION: Leek, tel 01538 483741

CYCLE HIRE: none near by

THE PUB: The Abbey Inn, Leek, see Directions to the pub, page 27

🛈 Take care along the banks of the lake – keep well away from the shore line

Getting to the start

From Leek take the A523 north west towards Macclesfield. Soon turn left on to the B5331, signed to Rudyard Lake. The entrance to the car park is on the left immediately under the railway bridge and before Rudyard village.

Why do this cycle ride?

Rudyard Lake is surrounded by wooded hills, pleasant hay meadows and cow pastures. The route takes full advantage of the countryside and offers opportunities to enjoy the other summertime facilities here such as a miniature railway, boat trips on the lake and rowing boat hire. It's an ideal family day out.

Researched and written by: Neil Coates

Rudyard Lake

STAFFORDSHIRE

2 Return to the old railway and carry on cycling northwards. The **lake** is easily visible through the trees – some care is needed as parts of the bank are prone to collapse, so keep well away from the shoreline. Looking across the lake, you'll see some of the odd boathouses that so delighted their owners a century and more ago. The lake is a popular place with school groups and Sea Scouts, so may well be lively with dinghies and Canadian canoes.

3 Passing by an intermediate railway halt, our route reaches the terminus of the miniature railway at **Hunthouse Wood**. More of the shore remains to be followed, however, so continue northwards along the old track, shortly passing through a gateway and on to a wider base of potholed, compacted ballast and cinders. The lake gradually narrows to its northern tip where there is a small **car park** and turning area. You can turn around here and retrace the route back to the start for a total ride length of 4 miles (6.4km). Before doing so it is worth diverting left along the tarred access lane for 200yds (183m) to a viewpoint offering a panorama down the length of the lake. The bridge here is across the canal feeder leat, which gathers Dingle Brook beyond the reedy marsh to the north. American troops trained for the D-Day landings in 1944 in this area, while the cornfields and pastures beyond were once a popular golf course.

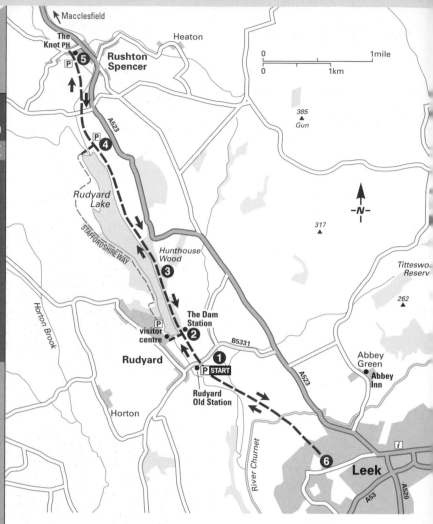

Macclesfield

The
Knot PH ⑤
P
Rushton
Spencer
Heaton

0   1mile
0   1km

385
▲
Gun

A523

P ④

Rudyard
Lake

317
▲

STAFFORDSHIRE WAY

–N–

Hunthouse
Wood

③

Titteswo
Reserv

262
▲

Horton Brook

P
visitor
centre

The Dam
Station
②

B5331

Rudyard

P START ①

Abbey
Green
● Abbey
Inn

A523

Rudyard
Old Station

Horton

River Churnet

i

⑥

Leek

A53

A520

④ Back on the old railway continue to the village of **Rushton Spencer**. Look to the right of the car park for wooden bollards and the muddy railway track. Take this (not the wider potholed road) through the trees, initially a muddy stretch that soon becomes a strip of compacted gravel on a grassy trail. This leads to the old station at Rushton Spencer. There's a superb North Staffordshire Railway station house here, and also a village pub called **The Knot.**

⑤ This is the end of the line; from here retrace your outward route back to **Rudyard Old Station**.

⑥ As a final flourish it is possible to follow the old trackbed south to the outskirts of **Leek,** just short of an old tunnel. This trip is beside pastureland and partly follows the route of the canal feeder leat and the little **River Churnet**. Return the same way back to Rudyard.

The Abbey Inn

about the pub

The Abbey Inn
Abbey Green Road, Leek
Staffordshire ST13 8SA
Tel 01538 382865
www.abbeyinn.co.uk

DIRECTIONS: The Abbey Inn is 1.75 miles (2.8km) from Rudyard Old Station. Take the B5331 and turn right on to the A523. In 300yds (274m) turn left along Highup Road, signed for Meerbrook, and continue to a T-junction where you turn right. The Abbey Inn is 0.5 miles (800m) on the left

PARKING: 40

OPEN: all day, closed Tuesday

FOOD: daily, all day Saturday and Sunday May–September

BREWERY/COMPANY: free house

REAL ALE: Bass, guest beer

ROOMS: 3 bedrooms

Set in beautiful countryside on the Staffordshire moorlands on the outskirts of Leek, this magnificent building enjoys an elevated position overlooking the infant Churnet Valley. It was built with stones recovered from the ruins of the nearby Cistercian Abbey of Dieu la Cresse and looks far older than its 1702 year of construction. Inside, head for the non-smoking snug bar, a super little room with bare sandstone walls, pine tables, collections of gleaming brass and copper jugs and pans, and tip-top Bass on tap. The main bar is spacious and comfortable, with a brick fireplace, photographs of old Leek town on the walls and a good mix of furnishings. From the front patio you have views along an elm-lined lane to the sandstone tower of Leek's parish church, and glimpses of the high moorlands to the north of town.

Food

From an extensive printed bar menu you can order hot filled baps, filled jacket potatoes and local favourites like oatcakes filled with cheese, and steak and mushroom pudding. Limited daily specials may include sweet and sour pork, tarragon chicken in white wine with mushrooms, and a range of fish dishes.

Family facilities

The Abbey Inn has a children's licence so they are welcome anywhere in the pub and they have a standard menu to choose from. There's also a good play area (slides, climbing ropes) adjacent to the garden.

Alternative refreshment stops

The Rudyard Hotel and a café and snack bar in Rudyard village.

☛ Where to go from here

In Macclesfield, to the north, visit Paradise Mill and the Silk Museum which together bring to life the industry that dominated the area during the Victorian era (www.silk-macclesfield.org).

Standedge from Marsden

A classic moorland ramble on the ancient Rapes Highway.

The Standedge Tunnel

Trans-Pennine travel has, until quite recently, been a hazardous business. Over the centuries many routes have been driven across the hills to link the industrial centres of West Yorkshire and Lancashire. Some paths were consolidated into paved causeways for packhorse traffic, before being upgraded to take vehicles. This track, linking the Colne Valley to the Lancashire towns of Rochdale and Milnrow, was known as the Rapes Highway.

This was tough terrain for building a canal. When the Huddersfield Narrow Canal was cut, to provide a link between Huddersfield and Ashton-under-Lyne, there was one major obstacle for the canal builders to overcome – the gritstone bulk of Standedge. The Standedge Tunnel, extending 3 miles (4.8km) from Marsden to Diggle, was a monumental feat of engineering. The result was the longest, highest and deepest canal tunnel in the country.

The tunnel was cut as narrow as possible, which left no room for a tow path. Towing horses had to be led over the hills to the far end of the tunnel, near Diggle in Lancashire. The bargees had to negotiate Standedge Tunnel using their own muscle power alone. This method, known as 'legging', required them to lie on their backs and push with their feet against the sides and roof of the tunnel. The canal was abandoned in 1944 but reopened in 2001. Seasonal boat trips into Standedge Tunnel are available from the visitor centre, 200yds (183m) from the tunnel portal.

the walk

1 From between the **Railway Inn** and the station, go left along the tow path of the **Huddersfield Narrow Canal**. At **Tunnel End** – where both canal and train lines disappear into a tunnel through the hillside – cross the canal on a footbridge, and walk up a track to the **Tunnel End Inn**.

2 Walk left along **Waters Road**. Keep straight ahead after 0.5 mile (800m), at the entrance to the **Hey Green Hotel**. 100yds (91m) further on, bear left, just before a cottage, on to a footpath. The path takes you across **Closegate Bridge**, known locally as **Eastergate Bridge**, where two becks meet.

3 Keep right, following the right-hand beck for about 100yds (91m), when the path bears left, up a steep side-valley. The path levels off at the top and then bears slightly right, towards the rounded prominence of **March Hill**. Your route across moorland is soon marked by a series of

what to look for

In spring and early summer, listen out for a cuckoo. If an old story is to be believed, the people of Marsden realised that when the cuckoo arrived, so did the sunshine. They tried to keep spring forever, by building a tower around the cuckoo. As the last stones were about to be laid, however, the cuckoo flew away. The good folk of Marsden use the joke against themselves, and now celebrate Cuckoo Day in April each year.

3h30 · **6.5 MILES** · **10.4 KM** · **LEVEL 2**

WALK

Marsden YORKSHIRE

waymarker stones, though your way ahead is unmistakable. After a few ups and downs, the path rises steeply uphill, before descending towards the A640.

4 Just before you reach the road, take a wooden bridge over a little beck and follow a **Pennine Way** sign on a track that bears acute left. Take this well-maintained gravel track uphill. After a few minutes you follow the contours of **Millstone Edge** and Standedge, a rocky ridge that offers panoramic views into **East Lancashire**. Just before the trig pillar is a plaque commemorating Amon Wrigley, a local poet.

5 Your route is downhill from here. Take a succession of stiles (some broken) in walls and fences before going left on an unmade road signposted **'Pennine Bridleway'** that leads down to the A62, where a car park overlooks **Brunclough Reservoir**.

6 Cross the road and take steps up to the left of the car park, signposted **'Pennine Way'**, to access a good track, soon revealing views to the left of **Redbrook Reservoir** and **Pule Hill** beyond. At a marker stone 800yds (732m) beyond the National Trust estate boundary gate, the **Pennine Way** bears right. But your route – having made a small detour to cross a tiny beck –

Left: Marsden Canal, next to Tunnel End Canal. Right: Standedge Edge
Page 31: Pack Horse Bridge

MAP: OS Explorer OL21 South Pennines
START/FINISH: Railway pub; roadside parking near by, grid ref SE 048117
PATHS: old tracks and byways, canal tow path, 9 stiles and handgates
LANDSCAPE: heather moorland
PUBLIC TOILETS: Marsden, at start of walk
TOURIST INFORMATION: Holmfirth, tel 01484 222444
THE PUB: Railway Inn, Marsden, see Point **1** on route

❶ A lengthy route largely across open moorland. It is most suited to experienced family walkers and should not be attempted when low cloud, mist or snow is prevalent

Getting to the start

Marsden is on the A62 road between Oldham and Huddersfield. Follow the brown tourist signs for the Standedge Visitor Centre. There is roadside parking near the Railway Inn. The railway station is at the top of Station Road. Daily trains on the Manchester Victoria to Huddersfield/Wakefield service.

Researched and written by:
Neil Coates, John Morrison

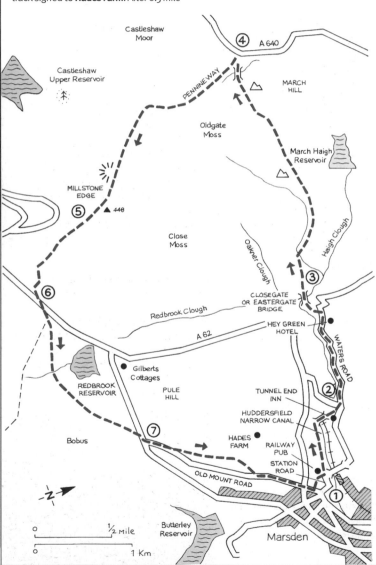

is to continue along the track. It gradually sweeps left, around the slopes of **Pule Hill**, to reach a road.

7 Turn right, along the road, but then immediately left, up **Old Mount Road**. After 100yds (91m), bear left again, up a stony track signed to **Hades Farm**. After 0.5 mile

(800m), take a path to the right, that accompanies a wall, to rejoin **Old Mount Road**. Follow the road downhill to arrive back in **Marsden**. Carefully cross straight over the A62, wind down to the junction beyond the church and bear left, uphill, to return to your car.

Castleshaw Moor

④ A 640

Castleshaw Upper Reservoir

PENNINE WAY

MARCH HILL

Oldgate Moss

March Haigh Reservoir

MILLSTONE EDGE

⑤ ▲ 448

Close Moss

Oakner Clough

Haigh Clough

⑥

Redbrook Clough

CLOSEGATE OR EASTERGATE BRIDGE

③

A 62

HEY GREEN HOTEL

WATERS ROAD

Gilberts Cottages

REDBROOK RESERVOIR

PULE HILL

TUNNEL END INN

②

HUDDERSFIELD NARROW CANAL

Bobus

⑦

HADES FARM

RAILWAY PUB

STATION ROAD

①

OLD MOUNT ROAD

Butterley Reservoir

Marsden

½ mile

1 Km

The Railway Inn

about the pub

The Railway Inn
Station Road, Marsden
Huddersfield, West Yorkshire
HD7 6DH
Tel 01484 841541

DIRECTIONS:	see Getting to the start
PARKING:	roadside parking
OPEN:	daily, all day
FOOD:	all day (until early evening on Sunday)
BREWERY/COMPANY:	Burtonwood
REAL ALE:	Burtonwood Bitter and Top Hat, guest beer
DOGS:	welcome throughout the pub

True to its name, this yellow-washed stone pub stands opposite the station and dates from about the same time – the 1840s. Beyond the sloping cobbled forecourt set with a few bench tables, flower tubs and shrubs, you will find a well maintained, open-plan interior with matching tables and chairs, fires, walls adorned with modern prints and traditional pub pictures, and unusual upholstered wall benches tucked into cosy corners. On sunny days visitors make the most of the sheltered back patio which looks out across the church to the high moors rising beyond.

Food
Straightforward pub food ranges from filled baked potatoes and home-made steak and ale pie on the printed menu to Cajun chicken and salmon fillet in tarragon butter on the short daily chalkboard choice.

Family facilities
Although there are few facilities for children they are welcome throughout the pub and they have their own menu to choose from. They will enjoy the patio on fine days.

Alternative refreshment stops
The Tunnel End Inn is on the route

☛ Where to go from here
The Saddleworth Museum and Art Gallery at Uppermill, south west of Marsden, is based in an old mill building next to the Huddersfield canal (www.saddleworthmuseum.co.uk).

The Jaws of Longdendale

The former Woodhead railway is the spine of a route that also includes reservoir roads amid the impressive scenery of Longdendale.

Rare mammals and UFOs

During the winter you may be lucky enough to see one of Britain's rarest mammals near Crowden. Unlike its lowland cousin, the mountain hare changes the colour of its coat during the winter. Gone is the familiar brown, its place taken by a coat of white fur. With a white coat and potentially several weeks, if not months, of snow, it is difficult to spot these creatures, and thus they escape the attention of predators. In spring the fur gradually moults and is replaced by the familiar brown coat giving the hares an unusual mottled look.

If cycling at dusk, keep an eye on the sky for the 'Longdendale Lights'. Mysterious lights in the sky have been reported here for decades, and the area is a favourite with British UFO spotters.

The lights may be those of aircraft turning over a beacon en route to Manchester airport, or even will-o'-the-wisps – phosphorescent lights resulting from the combustion of natural gases.

the ride

1 From the car park, walk your bicycle the short distance up to the **Longdendale Trail** and turn left. At this initial stage you're passing through immature woodland, one of an innovative series of 'Life for a Life' plantations in the Greater Manchester area, where a departed loved one can be

commemorated by the planting of a tree. The tree-lined route passes largely out of sight of **Torside Reservoir**, a popular venue for dinghy sailing, to reach the site of **Crowden Station**.

2 The two houses here are all that remain of the former railway, which was lifted amid great protest in the 1980s. Splendid views now open out up Longdendale, while above the far end of the dam is the little **Chapel of Ease**, **St James' Church**, where the victims of accidents and disease who died during the construction of the railway and reservoirs in the 1840s are buried in unmarked graves. The trackbed continues its easy, gentle climb eastwards just above the shoreline of **Woodhead Reservoir**.

3 This top reservoir narrows to a feeder stream, the infant **River Etherow**. Some miles downstream in **Stockport**, this combines with the rivers **Goyt** and **Tame** to form the **River Mersey**. The end of the line is reached at the **Woodhead Tunnels**. The latest, post-war bore was the last to be used by locomotives. The two earlier ones to the left are of a smaller diameter; one of them still has a narrow gauge railway disappearing into its depths. This allows engineers to service the power cables that have been routed beneath the **Pennines** here. High above, the notorious **Woodhead Pass Road** snakes across the hills. Time for a

Torside Reservoir is popular with water sports enthusiasts as well as cyclists and walkers

---

rest here before returning along the old railway. To your left are steep, heather -clad moors that are home to red grouse.

4 Returning to **Torside** you've completed 6 miles (9.7km). There's plenty more opportunity to the west however, so continue along the **Longdendale Trail** to a road crossing above the dam of **Torside Reservoir**. Take care crossing here. This is also where the **Pennine Way**, England's premier long-distance walk, is crossed. Pass high above **Rhodeswood Reservoir**, with views across to old hillside quarries now reclaimed by juniper woods. In about 0.75 mile (1.2km) reach a fingerpost giving a choice of routes. Turn right here (signed TPT West), go through a bridlegate and down a steep, gravelly path to a lane. Carefully cross this and take the even steeper rough track ahead (wheel your bikes here), leading to an undulating rough lane that eventually reaches the dam holding back **Valehouse Reservoir**. Cross this.

5 At the far side is a service road on the right. This is also a concessionary bridleway, so go through the gates and trace this level, tarred lane alongside the reservoir, the waters often obscured by pleasant woodlands. Beyond the lodge house the lane steepens around a series of bends to reach the next dam.

6 Cross this, **Rhodeswood Dam**, to a gate on the left signed for the **Longdendale Trail**. This steep track rises to an open gateway where you turn right up a narrower track to a bridlegate on the left. Take this to access the trackbed and turn left to return to the start.

| 3h30 | 11.5 MILES | 18.5 KM | LEVEL 2 |

SHORTER ALTERNATIVE ROUTE

| 1h30 | 6 MILES | 9.7 KM | LEVEL 1 |

MAP: OS Explorer OL1 Dark Peak

START/FINISH: Torside car parking, grid ref SK 068999

TRAILS/TRACKS: old railway trackbed, reservoir access roads and tracks

LANDSCAPE: moorland valley with reservoirs and industrial heritage

PUBLIC TOILETS: at start

TOURIST INFORMATION: Glossop, tel 01457 855920

CYCLE HIRE: Longdendale Valley Cycles, Hadfield tel 01457 854672

THE PUB: The Queen's Arms, 1 Shepley Street, see Directions to the pub, page 35

🛑 Don't do this ride on a cold, wet day with an easterly wind, as this will be funnelled down the valley making riding unpleasant and difficult

Getting to the start

Torside car park is on the B6105 south of Torside Reservoir to the east of Manchester. From the A628, turn right on to the B6105 just past Crowden.

Why do this cycle ride?

In this great trough-like valley that cuts through the Dark Peak, a string of reservoirs were developed during Victorian times to supply Manchester. The route follows a reclaimed railway along the shores of the reservoirs, while a branch crosses one of the dams to incorporate a pleasant wooded waterside stretch.

Researched and written by: Neil Coates

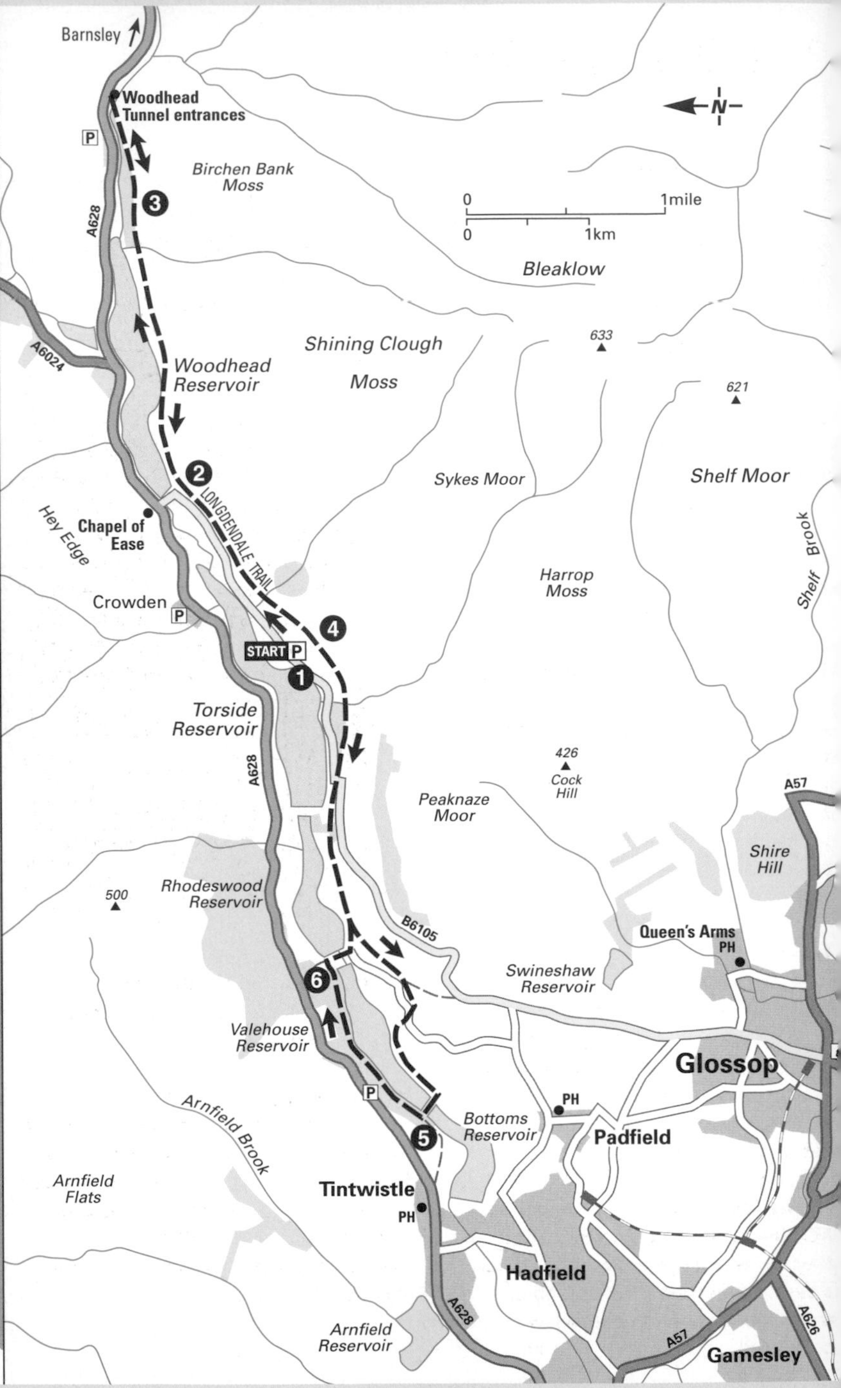

Barnsley

Woodhead
Tunnel entrances
P

Birchen Bank
Moss

Bleaklow

0   1mile
0   1km

A628

633 ▲

621 ▲

Woodhead
Reservoir

Shining Clough
Moss

Sykes Moor

Shelf Moor

Shelf Brook

A6024

Hey Edge

Chapel of
Ease

Crowden
P

LONGDENDALE TRAIL

Harrop
Moss

START P

Torside
Reservoir

A628

Peaknaze
Moor

426 ▲
Cock
Hill

A57

Shire
Hill

Rhodeswood
Reservoir

500 ▲

B6105

Swineshaw
Reservoir

Queen's Arms
PH

Glossop

Valehouse
Reservoir

P

Bottoms
Reservoir

PH

Padfield

Arnfield Brook

Tintwistle
PH

Hadfield

Arnfield
Flats

A628

A57

Arnfield
Reservoir

A626

Gamesley

The Queen's Arms

At the heart of a web of back lanes and passages that wind between the church, village cross and the nearby Manor Park, this is a splendid little pub in the picture-postcard village of Old Glossop. Hemmed in by fine old gritstone cottages, it's a solid street corner local with climbing roses and hanging baskets adding a splash of colour to the light stone exterior. The small taproom oozes character with darkwood panelling, deep upholstered wall benches, sporting prints on the walls, and eye-catching leaded glass windows. The low-beamed and carpeted L-shaped main bar is primarily laid up for dining, although drinkers are welcome here. There is a great range of real ales with changing guest beers.

about the pub

The Queen's Arms
1 Shepley Street, Old Glossop
Derbyshire SK13 7RZ
Tel 01457 862451

DIRECTIONS: The Queen's Arms is about 4 miles (6.4km) from Torside Car Park. Load the bikes on the car and turn left out of the car park on to the B6105 towards Glossop. In about 3 miles (4.8km), on a long downhill stretch into the outskirts of Glossop, pass the turn for the cemetery (right) and shortly turn left into Church Street. Pass the church, then bend right, and downhill, to find the pub on the left at a junction

PARKING: good on-street parking

OPEN: daily, all day

FOOD: daily, all day

BREWERY/COMPANY: Innspired

REAL ALE: Black Sheep Bitter, Worthington, 3 guest beers

Longdendale   DERBYSHIRE

Food
Expect to find a standard printed menu listing pub favourites – roast chicken, gammon, steak and kidney pie – and an ever-changing blackboard listing the likes of braised steak, lamb Henry and vegetable lasagne. Good value Sunday lunches; separate restaurant menu.

Family facilities
Although facilities are limited for children they are welcome away from the bar and a basic children's menu is available. Outdoor seating is limited to a few benches along the front of the pub.

Alternative refreshment stops
There is a part-time snack bar at Torside Visitor Centre.

☛ Where to go from here
In Stockport town centre are the fascinating Air Raid Shelters, a warren of tunnels hewn into the sandstone cliffs above the Mersey into which the townsfolk and millworkers could retreat during the Blitz (www.stockport.gov.uk and follow the links in Leisure and Culture).

Hayfield and the Sett Valley Trail

To Lantern Pike and Middle Moor above the Sett Valley above Hayfield.

On the Moorland's edge

Hayfield was busy. It had cotton mills, papermaking mills and calico printing and dye factories. Hayfield also had times of trouble. Floods washed away three bridges, even swept away some bodies from their churchyard graves. And in 1830 it resounded to marching feet of a thousand protesting mill workers demanding a living wage. Their industry went into a slow decline that would last a century, and Hayfield returned to its countryside ways.

The first part of the walk to little Lantern Pike follows the Sett Valley Trail, the trackbed of a railway that until 1970 linked Manchester and New Mills with Hayfield. At its peak the steam train would have brought thousands of people from Manchester. Today it's a pleasant tree-lined

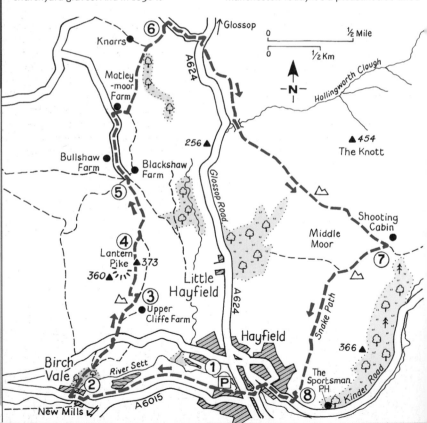

| 4h00 | 7 MILES | 11.3 KM | LEVEL 2 |

track, working its way through the valley between the hills of Lantern Pike and Chinley Churn. The track, and its former wasteland surroundings, are becoming a haven for wildlife. Beneath the ash, sycamore, beech and oak you'll see wood anemone, bluebells and wild garlic along with the rhubarb-like butterbur.

Lantern Pike is the middle of three ridges peeping through the trees, and by the time you get to Birch Vale you're ready to tackle it. You ascend on a shady path through woods, then a country lane with wild flowers in the verges, and finally on heather and grass slopes to the rocky summit. Having descended back to the busy Glossop road the route climbs across Middle Moor where it enters a new landscape of expansive heather fields. Soon you're on the skyline looking down on the Kinder and the green valley below.

You return to Hayfield on the Snake Path, an old traders' route linking the Sett and Woodland valleys. A fine street of stone-built cottages takes you to the centre.

Hayfield, on the lower slopes of Lantern Pike, shows little evidence of its former industrial life

MAP: OS Explorer OL1 Dark Peak
START/FINISH: Sett Valley Trail pay car park, Hayfield, grid ref SK 036869
PATHS: good paths and tracks, 12 stiles and gates
LANDSCAPE: heather moorland, rolling farm pastures
PUBLIC TOILETS: at car park
TOURIST INFORMATION: Glossop, tel 01457 855920
THE PUB: The Sportsman, Kinder Road, off Point **8** on route

🅗 This is a lengthy moorland walk and best suited to older children. The section across Middle Moor, towards the end of the route, may be muddy in places, especially in winter

Getting to the start

Hayfield is on the A624 between Glossop and Chapel-en-le-Frith. The main car park is signposted off the A624; turn off the village bypass on to the A6015 at the sign for New Mills.

Researched and written by:
Neil Coates, John Gillham

the walk

1 Follow the old railway trackbed signposted '**The Sett Valley Trail**', from the western end of the car park in Hayfield. This heads west down the valley and above the River Sett to meet the A6015 New Mills road at **Birch Vale**.

2 Turn right along the road, then right again along a cobbled track behind the cottages of the **Crescent** into the shade of woods. Beyond a gate, the track meets a tarred farm lane at a hairpin bend. Follow the higher course to reach a country lane. Staggered to the right across it, a tarred bridleway climbs further up the hillside. Take the left fork near **Upper Cliffe Farm** to a gate at the edge of the National Trust's **Lantern Pike** site.

3 Leave the bridleway here and turn left along a grassy wallside path climbing heather and bracken slopes to the rock-fringed ridge. Turn right and climb the airy crest to **Lantern Pike**'s summit, which is topped by a view indicator.

4 The path continues northwards from the top of Lantern Pike, descending to a gate at the northern boundary of the National Trust estate, where it rejoins the track you left earlier. Beyond a gate, bear gradually left across rushy pasture to a five-finger guidepost.

5 Bear left along the farm road and follow the main track for nearly 0.5 mile (800m) to the isolated **Matleymoor Farm**. Turn right across the foot of the farmyard on to a rough lane. Where this lane swings to the right leave it for a rough grassy track on the left. Go over the stile at its end and continue northwards on a grooved path, which joins a rough track from **Knarrs** 200yds (182m) beyond a stile. Turn right along this to reach a minor road.

6 Turn right along the road to reach the A624 road. Cross this with care and go over the stile at the far side. Turn immediately right, following a faint, rutted track with a wall on the right-hand side. This crosses the little valley of **Hollingworth Clough** on a footbridge before climbing up the heather slopes of **Middle Moor**.

7 About 150yds (137m) past a wooden causeway turn right at a signboard along the wide, stony **Snake Path**. Use the small kissing gate beside a gate and in 100yds (91m) keep left at a fork. A series of kissing gates and stiles takes the obvious route down to **Kinder Road** at the edge of **Hayfield**.

8 Turn right down the lane, then in 500yds (460m) go left down steps to emerge beside the **Royal Hotel**. Cross the nearby river bridge on **Church Street** and then go right down a side street signed to the **Sett Valley Trail**. This leads to the busy main road. Cross with care back to the car park.

what to look for

Lantern Pike was donated to the National Trust in 1950, after being purchased by subscription. It was to be a memorial to Edwin Royce, who fought for the freedom to roam these hills. A summit view indicator, commemorating Royce's life and struggle, records the 360 degree panorama.
Take a look round Hayfield. It has many old houses, former mills and cottages. Look out for The Pack Horse Inn on Kinder Road which dates back to 1577, and The Royal Hotel which was visited by John Wesley in 1755 – but in those days it was still the local parsonage.

The Sportsman

Standing in the wooded Sett Valley at the foot of Kinder Scout, this comfortable family-run inn is an obvious watering hole for those tackling the popular Kinder Scout Trail. It is a genuine old-fashioned hostelry created from a long terrace of stone houses. A warren of rooms radiates out from the central bar where the cosy, relaxed atmosphere is enhanced by heavy beams and timbers, crackling log fires in stone fireplaces, and old plates, sporting prints and shotguns adorning shelves and walls. A popular local, with pub games and plenty of room for drinkers in search of tip-top pints of Lancaster Bomber, it also draws customers who enjoy imaginative, freshly prepared food.

Food
Expect wholesome lunchtime snacks like ploughman's lunches, club sandwiches and filled baguettes alongside home-made soups (apple, celery and sherry) and chalkboard specials – fresh plaice, chicken breast braised in orange sauce, casseroled pork chops and apricot and almond tart.

Family facilities
Children are welcome inside and although there's no separate children's menu smaller portions of the main menu are available. There is a good garden and patio for fine weather eating and drinking.

Alternative refreshment stops
Twenty Trees Café or the Royal Hotel, both in Hayfield.

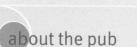

about the pub

The Sportsman
Kinder Road, Hayfield
Derbyshire SK12 5LE
Tel 01663 741565

DIRECTIONS: the pub is just off the route of the walk. You can either divert left at Point **8** – it's 0.25 mile (400m) to the pub – or finish the walk and drive there. Take the road through the village centre and turn up the narrow Kinder Road beside The Packhorse in Hayfield. Keep left to find the pub

PARKING: roadside parking

OPEN: daily, closed Monday lunchtime

FOOD: no food Sunday evening

BREWERY/COMPANY: Thwaites

REAL ALE: Thwaites Best and Thoroughbred, Lancaster Bomber

DOGS: welcome throughout pub

ROOMS: 6 bedrooms

☛ **Where to go from here**
In Stockport, to the west of Hayfield, visit the Hat Works or the Stockport Air Raid Shelters – a labyrinth of tunnels under the town centre (www.stockport.gov.uk and follow links for Leisure and Culture). Lyme Park (National Trust) is south of Disley off the A6 (www.nationaltrust.org.uk).

Into the Dark Peak

Explore the Sett Valley Trail before branching off along well-graded back lanes and the Pennine bridleway to the foot of the forbidding Kinder Scout.

Bowden Bridge Quarry

On the extension to the route up the Sett Valley you'll pass by Bowden Bridge Quarry. This commands a special place in the hearts of many ramblers and those who seek open access to England's higher and wilder places. In the 1920s there was a growing demand from people who lived in the towns and cities adjoining what is now the Peak District National Park, for the fresh air and freedom that the hills offered. These areas, the property of the wealthy classes and the preserve of those shooting grouse for a few weeks a year, were fiercely guarded by gamekeepers and staff employed to keep interlopers off these great estates. Minor confrontations and court cases bubbled on until the early 1930s, when things came to a head. On 24th April 1932 several hundred supporters of the 'right to roam' assembled at Bowden Bridge Quarry and set off for the moorlands of Kinder Scout, to assert a right to roam freely. They were soon confronted by estate staff determined to keep them off.

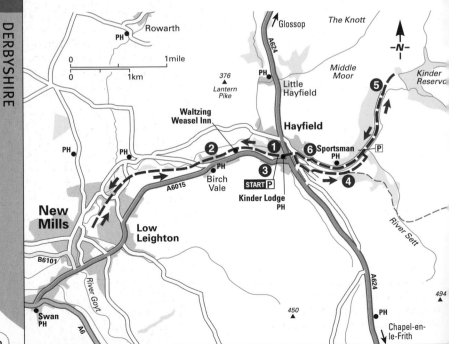

Kinder Downfall at Kinder Scout

The protest leaders were arrested and jailed. This action, which became known as the Mass Trespass, led to improvements to access and to today's national parks' system. On a busy Sunday, maybe 3,000 people would take the trains from Manchester to Hayfield Station to enjoy such hard-won freedoms. There's a plaque on the quarry wall recalling this seminal day.

the ride

1 The first stage is an easy ride along the trackbed of the former Hayfield to New Mills railway line that closed in the 1960s. Head away from the information and toilet block, following **'Sett Valley Trail'** signs

| 3h00 | 8.75 MILES | 14.1 KM | LEVEL 1 2 3 |

SHORTER ALTERNATIVE ROUTE

| 1h45 | 5 MILES | 8 KM | LEVEL 1 2 3 |

MAP: OS Explorer OL1 Dark Peak

START/FINISH: village car park at Hayfield Old Station, grid ref SK 037870

TRAILS/TRACKS: old railway trackbed, back lanes. One short footpath link where you walk your bicycle

LANDSCAPE: river valley woodlands with hill views; the extension has superb views to Kinder Scout plateau

PUBLIC TOILETS: Hayfield car park

TOURIST INFORMATION: Hayfield, tel 01663 746222

CYCLE HIRE: Old Station, Hayfield, tel 01663 746222

THE PUB: The Walzing Weasel Inn, Hayfield, just off the route

Getting to the start

Start from the Hayfield village car park signposted off the A624 Glossop to Chapel-en-le-Frith road. Turn on to the A6015 road for New Mills and then turn immediately right just after the Kinder Lodge pub.

Why do this cycle ride?

This simple there-and-back route, ideal for families with young children, passes through the lower Sett Valley. An extension to the route heads towards Kinder Scout along bridlepaths and reservoir roads, revealing excellent views and passing a famous marker along the way.

Researched and written by: Neil Coates

past the cycle hire centre. Once through a gateway a long, gentle descent takes the ride through the mature woodlands lining the old railway line. One section is a nature reserve; **Bluebell Wood** hints that a good time to visit is in May.

2 On the right, the mill lodge of one of countless local mills has been transformed into a fishery and is overshadowed by the hill of **Lantern Pike**. The trail bends to a roadside gate; don't take this but turn right to a lower gateway. Carefully cross the main road to the gateway opposite. The trail continues as an easy ride along a wooded course, crossing three more road crossings (all controlled by gates) to arrive abruptly at the end of the line, a gateway into **St George's Road** in **New Mills**. Turn here to retrace the route to the car park, a round trip of 5 miles (8km).

3 To extend the route along the **Sett Valley** and into the National Park, continue through the car park (signposted '**Kinder Trail**') and use the pedestrian-controlled lights to cross over the main road, keeping ahead to find the main village street. Turn right up this to reach the distinctively shaped old toll house near the hill crest. Fork left here, then immediately left again along **Valley Road**, signposted '**No Through Road**'. This quiet lane drops past cottages and houses to trace a course beside the lively **River Sett**. This is also the waymarked route of the new **Pennine Bridleway**.

4 Beyond the last cottages, you'll soon reach a parting of ways. The Pennine Bridleway is signed along a right fork, while a footpath is signed left along a wide path above the river. Dismount here and wheel your bicycle beside the water, shortly passing a footbridge to reach the **Peak Park Ranger Station** and a tarred access road. Pedal along this to **Bowden Bridge Quarry Car Park**. Turn right along the peaceful tarred lane. This undulates through woodland to arrive at a gateway into a service road to **Kinder Reservoir**. This is a concessionary bridleway, so pass through the gates and continue gently uphill to reach a turning area at the end of the road. It's well worth securing your bikes to rail fencing here and taking the very steep, cobbled bridlepath ahead-left a further 400yds (366m) to enjoy the views to **Kinder Downfall** (seasonal) waterfall and the surrounding hills.

5 Reclaim your bikes and return to **Bowden Bridge car park**. Remain on the lane here, soon passing by the **Sportsman** pub to reach the outskirts of **Hayfield**. The roads are narrow, so take care as you descend past cottages.

6 Ignore the first sharp left turn (**Spring Vale Road**); at the second a very short hill (**Bank Street**) drops you to the village centre. Turn left across the bridge, then right alongside the church to find the crossing back to the car park.

Birch Vale where you will find the Waltzing Weasel Inn

Waltzing Weasel Inn

CYCLE

Set within the heart of the Peak District, this traditional, 200-year-old country inn is popular with walkers and business people alike – no music or machines and no mobile phones permitted. Country antiques, carved oak pews and settles, stripped old tables, Victorian sporting prints, and a huge stone fireplace with roaring log fires in winter are impressive features of the cosy bar, while from the secluded terrace and garden and the mullion-windowed restaurant there are dramatic views of Kinder Scout. It's all very quiet, peaceful and homely, with the added attractions of good beer, decent wines and above average pub food.

Food

A solidly English bar menu is supplemented by daily dishes inspired by the owners' love of Italy. You'll find sandwiches, home-made soups, freshly baked pizzas, Peak pie and fish of the day, and there's always a hearty stew or casserole. There is a good range of vegetarian meals plus a set evening menu in the restaurant and popular Sunday roast lunches.

about the pub

Waltzing Weasel Inn
New Mills Road, Birch Vale
High Peak, Derbyshire SK22 1BT
Tel 01663 743402
www.w-weasel.co.uk

DIRECTIONS: 0.5 miles (800m) from Hayfield along the A6015 towards New Mills	
PARKING: 30	
OPEN: daily	
FOOD: daily	
BREWERY/COMPANY: free house	
REAL ALE: Marston's Best, Ruddles Best, guest beer	
ROOMS: 5 en suite	

Family facilities

Although there are no specific facilities for children they are welcome inside the pub and small portions of most main dishes are available. From the enclosed patio garden to the side there are good views for summer eating and drinking.

Alternative refreshment stops

There are plenty of pubs, cafés and restaurants in Hayfield.

☛ Where to go from here

The Chestnut Centre Wildlife Park near Chapel-en-le-Frith specialises in rare mammals and birds, such as otters and owls, from Britain, Europe and beyond (www.ottersandowls.co.uk).

Hayfield

DERBYSHIRE

Flash Village

Rogues, vagabonds and counterfeiters meet the righteous in England's highest village.

Flash

At an altitude of 1,518ft (463m), the village of Flash proclaims itself as the 'Highest Village in Britain', and at this elevation winter comes early and lingers past the point where spring has visited its lower neighbours. Winters here can be cold. Once, during wartime, it got so cold that the vicar had icicles on his ears when he ventured from his house to the church. On another occasion a visiting minister arrived by motorcycle. The congregation were surprised to see him because heavy snow was imminent. They told him to watch for it falling at the window opposite his pulpit and that, should he see any, he should stop the service and depart immediately. Just after he left, it started to snow and within 20 minutes the village was cut off.

Despite being a devout community, Flash also has the dubious honour of giving its name to sharp practice. The terms 'flash money' and 'flash company' entered the English language as a consequence of events in Flash. A group of peddlers living near the village, travelled the country hawking ribbons, buttons and goods made in nearby Leek. Known as 'Flash men' they initially paid for their goods with hard cash but after establishing credit, vanished with the goods and moved on to another supplier. Their name became associated with ne'er-do-wells in taverns, who helped people drink their money and were never seen again.

Flash money on the other hand was counterfeit, manufactured in the 18th century by a local gang using button presses. They were captured when a servant girl exposed them. Some of the gang members were hanged at Chester.

the walk

1 Walk through the village, pass the **pub** and an old **chapel**. Turn right at a footpath sign and head towards the last house. Go over a stile, turn right and follow the path over two walls. Veer left towards

what to look for

Look for evidence of the network of packhorse trails on the moors covered by this walk. These ancient routes were used from medieval times to transport goods between communities. Packhorse trains could have anything up to 50 horses and were led by a man called a 'jagger' (their ponies were Galloway cross breeds called Jaegers). Today you will find their paved routes across the moors, descending into the valleys in distinctive 'hollow ways' or sunken lanes. Jaggers still drove their hard-working beasts across the moors until the early 19th century, when canal transport finally usurped these HGVs of their day.

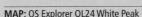

4h00 · **6 MILES** · **9.7 KM** · **LEVEL 1 2**

WALK

Flash Village

STAFFORDSHIRE

MAP: OS Explorer OL24 White Peak

START/FINISH: Flash village; parking on roadside near school, grid ref SK 026672

PATHS: some on road but mostly footpaths which can be boggy in wet weather. Around 35 stiles and gates

LANDSCAPE: hills, moorland and meadows

PUBLIC TOILETS: none on route

TOURIST INFORMATION: Buxton, tel 01298 25106

THE PUB: Traveller's Rest, Flash, see Directions to the pub, page 47

❶ The route explores a relatively remote area of the National Park and should not be attempted in bad weather, especially in low cloud or mist. Suitable for adventurous older children/family groups

Getting to the start

The village of Flash is off the A53 between Buxton and Leek. Drive south from Buxton for just over 4 miles (6.4km) passing the Travellers' Rest pub on your left. In a further 0.25 mile (400m), fork right on to a minor road to Flash. Park with care on the roadside before the school.

Researched and written by: Neil Coates, Moira McCrossan, Hugh Taylor

a gate in the corner of the field to a lane between walls. Follow this for 200yds (183m) then turn left at a waymarker along another walled track.

2 Continue through a gate then follow the waymarker right and uphill to **Wolf Edge**. Pass the rocks, veer left downhill over a stile and across heather moorland. Cross a stile on the right and continue downhill to a marker post. Cross the wall, then a bridge and turn left on to the road. Where the road forks keep right and continue through **Knotbury** then, after the last house on the left (Knotbury Lea), take the path on the left. Walk beside a wall. Where this bends left, go ahead and bear right to two nearby stiles. Turn left beside the fence past the second stile to find another stile, then go ahead on a path through heather to a further stile.

3 Follow the path down across moorland to join a ledged path through gnarled oakwoods before dropping on to a sandy bridleway. Turn left, veer right off the track at the next waymarker along a narrow path that leads to a stony farm lane. Turn left along this. At a bend beyond an open

Left: Rushton Spencer at the western edge of the Peak District National Park

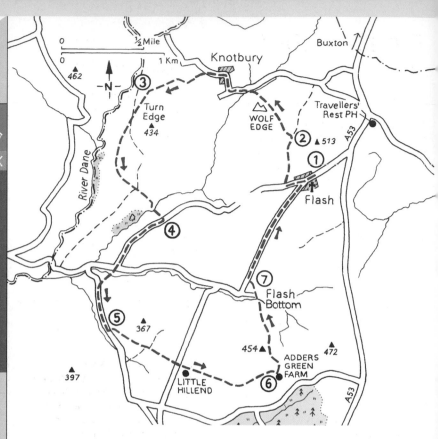

gateway leave this lane at a fingerpost along a faint green field road. Cross a stile then keep straight ahead at the next signpost. Follow this track until it crosses a hidden bridge over a stream (look carefully left for this), then climb steeply uphill to a barn and a lane.

4 Turn right. At the junction, turn right then left through a gap stile. Go downhill, over a bridge then uphill, following the path gradually left across the field to a gap stile. Here, turn left up the road and pass a house.

5 Go left at the next fingerpost, following the waymarked path to a farm track. At farm buildings go through a gate then fork

right. Continue to the road, cross it then continue on the path through **Little Hillend**. Follow this waymarked path to **Adders Green Farm**.

6 Turn left through a gate signed to **Flash Bottom** and alongside a wall. At the end of the wall turn left, follow the wall, cross a gate then follow the path round the foot of the hill. Aim to pass left of the small plantation, cross a flat bridge to a small gate, turn left and go over a stile into a farm drive.

7 Cross a stile opposite, follow the path over a field and up steps left of the house to the road. Turn right and walk this quiet road back up to **Flash**.

Travellers' Rest

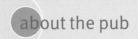
about the pub

Travellers' Rest
Flash, Quarnford, Buxton
Derbyshire SK17 0SN
Tel 01298 23695

DIRECTIONS: the pub is beside the A53, a mile (1.6km) from Flash village and the start of the walk	
PARKING: 40	
OPEN: all day Saturday and Sunday, closed Monday	
FOOD: daily (except Monday)	
BREWERY/COMPANY: free house	
REAL ALE: Tetley, Marston's Pedigree and Hartington IPA	
DOGS: welcome on a lead	

The Travellers' Rest, one of the highest pubs in England, is set back from the main road and enjoys grand views to the nearby moorland gritstone edges and across rolling pastures to the White Peak. Built of local stone some 250 years ago, it's a rambling place with a warren of small rooms leading off a central wooden bar. Expect heavy beams, grand old fireplaces with blazing log fires, and old tables and chairs. The walls are covered with clocks, and shelves and windowsills display old scales and stone jars, while ceilings are hung with farming implements and horse tack. Walkers can be assured of a warm welcome.

Food

All meals are home cooked using fresh local produce whenever possible. Pub favourites include fish and chips and steak and Guinness pie, with daily blackboard dishes like beef in port and Stilton, liver and bacon in red wine, and mango and ginger chicken. Lighter lunchtime snacks are available.

Family facilities

Children are welcome and they will love the museum-like interior. There's a standard children's menu and on fine days you can make use of the patio which offers extensive valley views.

Alternative refreshment stops

The New Inn in Flash village centre or drive north to Buxton where there are plenty of options.

☛ Where to go from here

After the walk take a short pony trek (over 8s only) from Northfield Farm in Flash village. You must book in advance for this (www.northfieldfarm.co.uk), or visit the former spa town of Buxton (www.visitbuxton.co.uk).

Combs Reservoir and Dickie's Meadow

A quiet corner of Derbyshire, between the Goyt and Chapel-en-le-Frith.

Combs Reservoir

Combs lies in a quiet corner of north west Derbyshire beneath the sombre crag-fringed slopes of Combs Moss. The route starts by the west side of the dam on a narrow path between the lake and Meveril Brook. Red campion, and thickets of dog rose line the path, which rounds the reservoir to its

southern tip. Beyond the reservoir the path tucks under the railway, which brings to mind a story concerning Ned Dixon, who lived in nearby Tunstead Farm. Ned, or Dickie as he was known, was murdered by his cousin. Locals say his spirit lived on in his skull, which was left outside to guard against intruders. Strange things were said to happen when anybody tried to remove the skull. It is also claimed that the present road from Combs to Chapel was built because the railway bridge would not stand over Dane Hey Road. After the first bridge

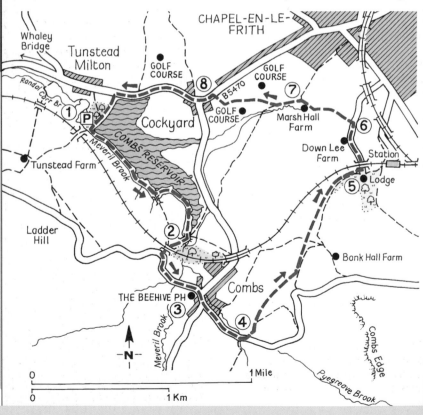

Combs

DERBYSHIRE

was completed it collapsed, burying the workmen's tools. This was blamed on the skull: Dickie had been against the railway going across Tunstead land.

A lane with hedges of honeysuckle and hawthorn winds into the village of Combs, where a handful of stone-built cottages are centred on the Beehive Inn. Combs' most famous son is Herbert Froode. He made his name in automotive engineering as one of the inventors of the brake lining. In the early 1890s he developed woven cotton brakes for horse drawn wagons, but his ideas didn't really take off until 1897 when the first motor buses emerged. By the end of the century Froode had won a contract to supply brake linings for the new London omnibuses. Through the village the route takes to the hillsides. Now Combs Reservoir, which is spread beneath your feet, looks every bit a natural lake. Beyond it are the plains of Manchester and the hazy blue West Pennine horizon. In the other direction the gritstone cliffs of Combs Edge overshadow the sullen combe of Pyegreave Brook. This pleasing walk ends as it starts, by the shores of the reservoir. If you look along the line of the dam towards the right of two farms, you'll see where Dickie lived.

MAP: OS Explorer OL24 White Peak
START/FINISH: Combs Reservoir car park, grid ref SK 033797
PATHS: can be muddy, 14 stiles and gates
LANDSCAPE: lakes, meadows and high moors
PUBLIC TOILETS: none on route
TOURIST INFORMATION: Buxton, tel 01298 25106
THE PUB: The Beehive Inn, Combs see Point **3** on route

Getting to the start

The car park at Combs Reservoir is in the village of Tunstead Milton, about 2 miles (3.2km) south east of Whaley Bridge on the B5470 towards Chapel-en-le-Frith. Look on the right for a no-through road sign, a small lodge and a British Waterways board for the reservoir; the car park is at the western end of the dam.

Researched and written by: Neil Coates, John Gillham

Combs Reservoir

the walk

1 From the dam take the path, initially concreted, between the reservoir and Meveril Brook. Ignore the first footbridge at a corner.

2 As the reservoir narrows the path traverses small fields, then comes to another footbridge on your right over the brook. This time cross it and head south

Combs

DERBYSHIRE

across another field. Beyond a foot tunnel under the Buxton line railway, the path reaches a narrow hedge-lined country lane. Turn left along the lane into **Combs** village.

3 Past the Beehive Inn in the village centre, take the lane straight ahead, then the left fork, signposted '**Dove Holes**'. This climbs out of the village towards Combs Edge.

4 Take the second footpath on the left, which begins at a muddy clearing on the left just beyond **Millway Cottage**. Go through the stile and climb on a partially slabbed path through a narrow grassy enclosure. After 100yds (91m) put a wall on your right and climb the pastured spur overlooking the huge combe of **Pygreave Brook**. Go through a gateway and then a stile in the next two boundary walls before following a wall on the right. Ignore a gate in this wall – that's a path to **Bank Hall Farm**, but stay with the narrow path raking across rough grassy hillslopes with the railway line and the reservoir below left. Take the next stile rather than the handgate, gradually losing height.

5 The path descends to a track alongside the railway. This joins a lane just short of the **Lodge**. Turn left to go under the railway and north to **Down Lee Farm**.

6 Turn left through a kissing gate 100yds (91m) beyond the farmhouse. The path follows an overgrown hedge towards **Marsh Hall Farm**. The fields can become very

what to look for

On a bright winter's day in 1995 a group of birdwatchers, wandering by the hedge along the west shores of the reservoir, came across some huge clawed footprints 3.5ins (89mm) wide, which were sunk deep into the mud. After studying the photographs they had taken, it became obvious that a huge cat had been on the prowl – probably the infamous Peak Panther that has had many sightings on the nearby hills above Chinley and Hayfield.

boggy on the final approaches. When you reach the farm complex turn right over a stile beside a house and join a driveway left of the stone dovecote.

7 After 100yds (91m) take a stile, left, then another and walk to a stile at the edge of **Chapel-en-le-Frith golf course**. Head almost straight ahead, aiming for the red-roofed house beyond fairways. Look for a stile 200yds (182m) before this and cross a small field to the B5470.

8 Turn left along the road (there's a pavement on the far side), and follow it past the **Hanging Gate pub** at **Cockyard**. After passing the entrance to the sailing club, turn left to cross the foot of the dam of Combs Reservoir and return to the car park at the start of the walk.

Walking along the shore of Combs Reservoir

The Beehive Inn

about the pub

The Beehive Inn
Combs, High Peak
Derbyshire SK33 9UT
Tel 01298 812758
www.thebeehiveinn.co.uk

DIRECTIONS: The Beehive is at Point 3 of
the walk. If driving there from the parking
area at Combs Reservoir, turn right along the
B5470, then right again at Cockyard
for Combs

PARKING: 25 and good roadside parking

OPEN: daily, all day Saturday and Sunday

FOOD: daily, all day Sunday

BREWERY/COMPANY: free house

REAL ALE: Boddingtons, Bass, Timothy
Taylor Landlord

DOGS: taproom and patio only

*Despite its off-the-beaten-track location
in an isolated rural hamlet, the stone-
built Beehive Inn really buzzes with
activity, drawing locals in on Tuesday
for the quiz night, music-lovers on Friday
for live sessions, and hordes of ramblers
throughout the week for generous home-
cooked food and first-rate beer. In winter
they cluster around the warming log
fires in the open-plan main bar with
its old pews and settles, refectory
and famhouse tables and bric-a-brac.
The popular village local also has a
separate taproom with simple benches.
In summer visitors spill out on to the
pretty paved patio.*

Food

Tuck into hearty Brie and bacon
sandwiches or try beer-battered black
pudding with creamy green peppercorn
sauce as a satisfying snack or starter.
Main meals might include steak and ale
pie, grilled chicken breast with mushroom
sauce, salad Niçoise or chicken curry.
A good value, three-course 'rapid menu'
is served from Monday to Friday.

Family facilities

Children are very welcome in the
main bar where they have their
own menu to choose from. There
is plenty of space on the front
patio for summer eating
and drinking.

Alternative refreshment stop

The more formal Hanging Gate
Inn is at Cockyard just before you
get back to the reservoir dam.

☛ **Where to go from here**
The Chestnut Centre Otter, Owl and Wildlife
Park is near Chapel-en-le-Frith. This wildlife
and conservation park is home to otters,
owls, a herd of fallow deer, Scottish wild
cats and foxes (www.ottersandowls.co.uk).

The Manifold Way

Manifold Valley

DERBYSHIRE/STAFFORDSHIRE

Follow the Manifold Way, former route of one of England's most picturesque small railways.

Leek and Manifold Valley Light Railway
Described by one local as 'A line starting nowhere and ending up at the same place'

the narrow gauge Leek and Manifold Valley Light Railway was one of England's most picturesque white elephants. Though it survived a mere 30 years from its first run in June 1904, its legacy is still enjoyed today. It ran for 8 miles (12.9km) from Hulme End to Waterhouses where passengers and freight had to transfer to the standard gauge Leek branch of the North Staffordshire Railway.

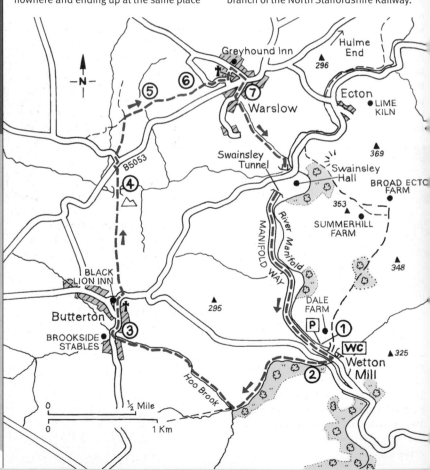

The success of the line was based on the supposition that the Ecton Copper Mines would reopen and that an extension to Buxton would tap into a lucrative tourist market. But the mines didn't reopen and the extension was never built. To survive, the small railway made a daily collection of milk from farms along the line and hauled produce from the creamery at Ecton for onward transportation to London. Tourists did flock to the area on summer weekends and bank holidays, often overloading the carriages as they headed for scenic areas like Thor's Cave and Beeston Tor. Even with this seasonal upturn the line never made a profit and when the creamery shut in 1933 it was the end of the road for the miniature trains. The last one ran on 10 March 1934.

The track was lifted and the bed presented by the railway company to Staffordshire County Council. They had the remarkable foresight and imagination to be one of the first local authorities to take a disused railway line and convert it to a pedestrian path. Today, as the Manifold Way, it is a favourite of walkers and cyclists.

Above: Old Field Lane

Map: OS Explorer OL24 White Peak

START/FINISH: on the Manifold Way near Wetton Mill Bridge, grid ref SK 095561

PATHS: hard surface on the Manifold Way, other footpaths can be muddy in wet weather

LANDSCAPE: woodland, meadows and valleys

PUBLIC TOILETS: at the tea room over Wetton Mill Bridge and at Warslow Village Hall

TOURIST INFORMATION: Leek, tel 01538 483741

THE PUB: The Greyhound, Leek Road, see Point 6 on route

🛑 Keep an eye on younger children on the final section between Swainsley Tunnel and Wetton Mill as the narrow road is shared with light traffic

Getting to the start

From the A523 between Leek and Ashbourne take the B5053 north towards Hartington. Turn right for Butterton and continue towards Wetton and Alstonefield. The car park is just north of Wetton Mill Bridge in the Manifold Valley.

Researched and written by: Neil Coates, Moira McCrossan, Hugh Taylor

Manifold Valley

DERBYSHIRE/STAFFORDSHIRE

what to look for

The walk passes through the one tunnel that served the old railway. This is close to Swainsley Hall, which was the home of the Wardle family at the time of construction. They were shareholders in the company building the line and although happy to take any profits going did not want to be troubled by seeing the trains from their house.

the walk

1 From the car park just north of Wettonmill Bridge, walk past the bridge itself and turn right for **Butterton**. Ignore the fork left across a ford, and within a few paces take a gate on the left on to a waymarked bridleway, soon joining a field road.

2 Pass by a broken stile and bear left to cross a flat bridge, continuing upstream alongside **Hoo Brook**. Cross another stile above a hanging fence and remain by the water. In 0.5 mile (800m) cross a small footbridge, then turn right over a stile signed as a footpath to **Butterton**. Further upstream a fingerpost points left down to slippery stepping-stones across Hoo Brook, then more stones across a side stream. Remain beside Hoo Brook to re-cross it at the edge of **Butterton**, walking along the rough track to the village road.

3 Turn right at **Brookside Stables**, cross the footbridge above the long ford and keep right. In 250yds (229m) fork right on to a lane between the church and the **Black Lion Inn**. Bend right outside the churchyard wall and take the rough walled lane left. Follow this to a gate and stile beside a small barn. Keep ahead along a line of ash trees, go over a couple of stiles and across a steepening ridge end. Keep to the

immediate right of a reedy cleft and drop down a steep slope to cross the stream by a footbridge hidden beneath an alder tree.

4 Take the stile and walk right past an upright stone. Keeping the hedge on your left, rise to a lane. Turn right. Turn left for **Elkstone** then right in 100yds (91m) on to a footpath behind two hydrant markers. Cross two stiles, turn right behind a small derelict building and follow the line of the wall. Cross two stiles, then a stream (difficult and muddy) and head uphill, with a fence on your left.

5 As the fence turns left, fork half right across the field to a stile by a large tree. Follow the path through a gap in the hedge opposite, then aim left to the corner of the next field. Veer right from a derelict building, cross a difficult stile and head half left across marshy ground to two low stone posts.

6 Cross to a further two stones at the end of a hedgerow, go alongside the hedge (right) to a waymark pole and two stiles. Take the narrow stile ahead and walk to the barn left of the farm. Go through the farmyard and turn right along Back Lane. At the T-junction turn left to **Warslow** village and the **Greyhound Inn**. Turn right to reach the B5053.

7 Look right to find **School Lane**, cross the road to take this byroad. In 150yds (137m), go through a gap stile on the left. Clamber through more gap stiles, roughly following the course of a stream on the left. Take another stile just left of a ruinous barn, then a further stile. Enter a wooded area on a distinct path, eventually drop down on to the **Manifold Way** and turn right. Join a minor road passing through **Swainsley old railway tunnel** and remain on this back to the car park.

The Greyhound Inn

Close to the church in the heart of the village the Greyhound, which dates from 1750, is a solid stone building adorned with creepers, and hanging baskets and flower troughs in summer. Inside you'll find a basic taproom with an open fire, matchboard panelling, bare stone walls and beams hung with bed warmers, copper kettles and old lamps. The separate carpeted lounge bar has maroon and green wall coverings, antique oak settles and traditional pub tables and chairs, with greyhound paintings and old village photographs lining the walls. Add plenty of candles and a chatty atmosphere and you have a welcoming village local.

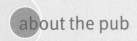

about the pub

The Greyhound Inn

Leek Road
Warslow, Buxton
Derbyshire SK17 0JN
Tel 01298 84249
www.thegreyhoundwarslow.co.uk

DIRECTIONS: Warslow village and the pub (near the church) are on the B5053 south of Buxton

PARKING: 25

OPEN: daily, all day Sunday. Closed Monday and Tuesday lunchtime October–Easter

FOOD: daily

BREWERY/COMPANY: free house

REAL ALE: Marston's Pedigree, Black Sheep Bitter, guest beers

DOGS: welcome inside

ROOMS: 4 bedrooms

Food

Expect a wide choice of good, home-cooked pub food listed on blackboards. From sandwiches, filled jacket potatoes and good ham, egg and chips, the choice extends to steak and ale pie, beef in red wine, chicken in a creamy cider sauce, pan-fried fresh tuna, and a selection of steaks.

Family facilities

Children are welcome throughout the pub and younger family members have a standard menu to choose from. The tree-shaded garden is a safe haven for children on fine days.

Alternative refreshment stops

The tea room at Wetton Mill is open most days in summer and many weekends in the winter months. The Black Lion Inn in Butterton is open some weekday lunchtimes and every evening.

☛ Where to go from here

The Manifold Valley Visitor Centre at Hulme End, just north of Ecton, has displays covering the history of the Leek and Manifold Light Railway. Blackbrook Zoological Park at Winkhill, near Leek, is home to rare birds, unusual animals, reptiles and insects (www.blackbrookzoologicalpark.co.uk).

Longnor and Hollinsclough

Ramble over hills and dales in the footsteps of television's fictitious doctors.

Peak Practice

Longnor, a charming Peak village, situated on a high ridge between the Dove and Manifold rivers, developed as a meeting place on the ancient trade routes that once crossed these hills from Sheffield, Chesterfield, Nottingham and the Potteries. More recently it has become famous as the location of the television drama *Peak Practice*, which chronicles the everyday lives of a group of country doctors and their patients. First screened in 1993, the series put Peak District scenery on the television

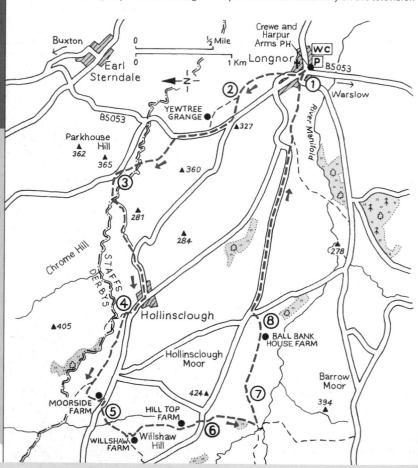

map and has attracted countless visitors. The earlier episodes took different parts of the area to establish fictional Cardale. However, the drama has now established a base in this Staffordshire village to give the programmes a permanent, community feel. Real life in Longnor, though, is somewhat quieter than the TV version.

There is plenty that will be familiar to viewers of *Peak Practice*. The fine brick frontage of the fictional Cardale Tearoom is actually a Georgian hotel built to serve the needs of the Crewe and Harpur Estate and still retains that name. It was used as a meeting place for the local farmers when they came to pay their annual rents at the end of March. The Horseshoe has the honour of being the TV doctors' local, the Black Swan. Dating back to 1609 it was an important staging point for the packhorse and carriage trade that crossed these hills. Ye Olde Cheshire Cheese, one of several other pubs in the village, had its origins as a cheese store in 1464.

The ancient pubs and cobbled market square are a reminder of Longnor's importance in days gone by as a market town. The turnpike roads with their tolls, and the lack of a railway link, prevented Longnor's development as a major trading centre, but the village retains its Victorian market hall. Now a craft centre and coffee shop, it still has the old market toll charge board, with a list of long-forgotten tariffs, above the front door. However Longnor's old world ambience and location at the heart of ancient paths ensures that it is still busy with walkers, cyclists and tourists.

Top: Parkhouse Hill
Right: The main street through Longnor

3h30 · **6 MILES** · **9.7 KM** · **LEVEL 2**

(11)

👫 **WALK**

MAP: OS Explorer OL24 White Peak

START/FINISH: Longnor market square, grid ref SK 089649

PATHS: some on road otherwise good footpaths, can be muddy. About 42 gates and stiles

LANDSCAPE: valleys, hills and meadows

PUBLIC TOILETS: Longnor market square

TOURIST INFORMATION: Buxton, tel 01298 25106

THE PUB: Crewe and Harpur Arms, Longnor, in market square at start of walk

❶ This is a lengthy, undulating walk best suited to older children

Getting to the start

Longnor is south of Buxton on the B5053. The easiest approach is to take the A53 from Buxton south towards Leek and turn off left at The Travellers' Rest pub at Quarnford (Flash). At the road junction immediately north of Longnor turn right to the market square where there is parking.

Researched and written by: Neil Coates, Moira McCrossan, Hugh Taylor

Longnor · STAFFORDSHIRE

what to look for

Well dressing is a centuries old Peak District tradition. A soaked wooden framework holds a bed of clay, into which flower petals, moss, berries, cones and seeds are pressed in an intricate design. The display is then placed over the well in a special ceremony. Each village has its own design and date. Dressings take place throughout the summer; Longnor's is around the first week in September.

the walk

1 From the market square take the road towards Buxton. In 150yds (137m) turn right into **Church Street**, then take the no-through road immediately left. In 100yds (91m) look right for steps leading up to a footpath. Follow the waymarkers, behind some houses, over a stile and along a wall. Cross another stile, go downhill and turn left on to a farm road.

2 Keep left at the renovated farm, rising to a road. Turn right, descend past the traffic lights and just before the bend fork left on a rough, waymarked drive. At the end of this continue through a gate on to a footpath, through a gap stile, downhill, across a bridge and continue straight ahead. Eventually cross a stile and turn left on to the road.

3 Fork left on to a farm road, following the waymarked path. Cross a footbridge by a ford and turn left, walking a field path by the stream to reach a road. Turn right through **Hollinsclough**, following the road to the right and uphill. Turn right on to a bridlepath, through a gate and downhill.

4 In 50yds (45m) fork left by two stones and continue along the flank of the hill for 0.5 mile (800m). At the point where the path divides into three at the top end of an old hawthorn hedge, fork left to pass by an old gatepost and go uphill on a wide track.

At the top turn left at a stone gatepost, go through **Moorside Farm** to reach a lane. Turn right to find a footpath on the left, opposite at house called 'The Glen'.

5 Walk downhill beside a reedy ditch. Cross to the left of this to find a stile leading on to a bushy bank dropping steeply to a stream. Cross this and walk directly upslope to a stile. Beyond this trace the faint field road to a gateway well right of **Willshaw Farm**. Turn back to the farm, go through the farmyard and then fork right at a fingerpost, walking ahead to another hillside path. Keep the old hedge on your left to pass a waymark post. At the steep gully turn right along a diverted footpath, crossing 2 stiles to reach the driveway to **Hill Top Farm** at a cattle grid. Take the stile opposite and keep ahead around the sloping field to a stile by a gate into a road.

6 Cross the road and take the farm road opposite. In 100yds (91m) at a stone dump, go right steeply downhill, over a stile and follow the path along the wall. Just before the first footbridge, cross a stile on the left and head uphill to the left of some trees.

7 Continue walking uphill, through a gate in a stone wall to some ruined buildings. Follow the track right, below these ruins through to **Ball Bank House Farm**. Bear left after two barns, then go left on to an indistinct footpath uphill, starting just behind the farmhouse.

8 At the top of the slope go through a stile, follow the wall uphill, over two stiles to the road. Turn left then right towards **Longnor**. Just before the road bends left, cross a stile on the right, go downhill and over a slab bridge, then through a squeeze stile, up to a corner squeeze stile and then further stiles to a farm road. Turn right to return to the village.

Crewe and Harpur Arms

This imposing, ivy-covered brick pub-hotel standing in Longnor's picturesque market square is named after a local landowning family. Within, it is comfortable, welcoming and well lived in with a popular bar offering Marston's ales on tap and a more formal lounge area sporting an open log fire, old pews, and walls decorated with brasses, plates, maps and local paintings. In summer visitors can enjoy alfresco seating on a sheltered paved patio and a lawned area, both with bench tables, and lovely views down the Manifold Valley and across the Dove Valley to the limestone hills and dales beyond.

about the pub

Crewe and Harpur Arms
Longnor, Buxton
Derbyshire SK17 0NG
Tel 01298 83205

DIRECTIONS: Longnor market square, see Getting to the start
PARKING: 90
OPEN: daily, all day Saturday and Sunday
FOOD: daily, all day Saturday and Sunday
BREWERY/COMPANY: Marston's
REAL ALE: Marston's Bitter and Pedigree, Timothy Taylor Landlord
DOGS: welcome in the bar (not overnight)
ROOMS: 7 en suite

Food
Expect good lunchtime snacks and an extensive main menu listing the likes of beef and ale casserole along with Brie, courgette and almond crumble and a range of steaks. Daily dishes could include chicken and bacon pie or salmon fillet in champagne sauce.

Family facilities
Children can let off steam in the play area in the garden. They are welcome indoors and have their own menu listing the usual favourites.

Alternative refreshment stops
The Manifold Chip Shop and Tearoom and the Frankley Scarlet Café are both in Longnor.

☛ Where to go from here
Take a ride on the Churnet Valley Railway which stops at the Victorian station at Cheddleton. Cheddleton also has two working water mills (www.churnet-valley-railway.co.uk).

Along the Manifold

12

Follow England's oldest multi-user trail on an easy ride through woodland, deep gorges and past spectacular caves above part-time rivers.

Disappearing rivers

If you enjoy this ride in the summer months, then mention of rivers may strike you as a mistake. There's no water to be seen in the first 4.5 miles (7.2km) of the route, and then only intermittently thereafter.

The reason is that the underlying rock is limestone and as this is extremely porous the water cannot, except in the wettest weather, maintain a flow at the surface. Instead, it trickles away down 'swallets' to carve a remarkable underground course through fissures, passages and caves which are not necessarily directly beneath the dry riverbeds.

Both the River Hamps and the Manifold exhibit this characteristic. Their combined waters eventually resurface in the National Trust's estate at Ilam, a few miles towards Ashbourne. In place of the water are rivers of green. These are the enormous leaves of butterbur, which thrive in damp places and can survive the occasional flood of water after a particularly heavy downpour. It's at Dafar Bridge, just before you reach Wettonmill, that the waters are seen permanently at the surface. At the series of swallets here, an eccentric Edwardian spent a fortune burying iron pipes into the river bed in an attempt to create real 'Water Music' by means of differing pressures as the water disappeared underground. Success was elusive!

the ride

1 The signal box at the old station is the starting point. The station itself was an interchange between the standard gauge line to Leek and the narrow gauge Leek and Manifold Light Railway. This 2ft 6in gauge line meandered through these remote valleys between 1904 and 1934, and this is the route we now follow. The ride soon joins a wide cycle-pavement beside the main road. On reaching the crossing point, carefully cross into the 'No Traffic' lane opposite. You'll immediately cross a bridge over the **River Hamps**, one of many such crossings in the next few miles. It's an easy trip along the tarred way, curving this way and that towards the enclosing valley sides.

2 Soon after **Lee House Farm** is passed (teas and meals here in season) the ash woods close in and the route becomes tunnel-like beneath these bird-rich boughs. In 2 miles (3.2km) the route curves gradually left to reveal **Beeston Tor**. In the caravan field on your right here, note the old green hut, the former refreshment room of Beeston Tor Station. Here, also, the Hamps meets with the River Manifold, flowing south beneath the Tor towards the distant River Dove. The route now runs parallel to an access road before reaching a gateway and a lane at **Weag's Bridge**.

3 Carefully cross straight over and ride through the car park to and through the gate at the end, regaining a non-trafficked

The imposing site of Thor's Cave

stretch. This is probably the most spectacular part of the valley, the river gyrating between immensely steep cliffs cloaked in some of England's finest ash woods. As the route leaves the trees around a left-hand curve, stop to look back to see the awesome location of **Thor's Cave**, high above the valley. An interpretation board tells its history; a steep path leads up to it.

4 The tortuous road between Wetton and Grindon is soon reached at a gated bridge. Beyond here, and for the next 3 miles (4.8km), you will share the road with other traffic, so care is needed. It's easier to continue ahead along the flatter route marking the old railway (the other road here loops back in after 0.5 miles/800m) to reach the popular tea rooms at **Wetton Mill**. Beware of traffic here at another minor junction. This is a good place to turn around if you are taking the shorter alternative route (9 miles/14.5km round trip).

5 Continuing north, the road keeps company with the river to reach **Swainsley Tunnel**. This is shared with vehicles, but is wide enough for bike and car and also well lit. At the far end go ahead back on to a segregated track, cycling north to pass beneath bald **Ecton Hill** and its sombre mining remains. Crossing another road here, the valley sides gradually pull back for the final approach to journey's end, the station at **Hulme End**.

6 Turn around here and retrace your route back to the start. Take care at **Weag's Bridge** to take the gated lane rather than the access road to the caravan site at Beeston Tor Farm.

MAP: OS Explorer OL24 White Peak
START/FINISH: Waterhouses Old Station, grid ref SK 085503
TRAILS/TRACKS: the entire route is tarred, some of it badly pitted, about 3 miles (4.8km) is shared with light road traffic, one tunnel
LANDSCAPE: limestone gorges, ash woods and good views towards the moorlands
PUBLIC TOILETS: Waterhouses and Hulme End stations.
TOURIST INFORMATION: Leek, tel 01538 483741
CYCLE HIRE: Waterhouses Old Station, tel 01538 308609; also Brown End Farm, tel 01538 308313
THE PUB: Ye Olde Crown Hotel, Waterhouses, near Point **1** on route

Getting to the start

Waterhouses Old Station is in the village of Waterhouses, on the A523 about half-way between Leek and Ashbourne. Turn up the road beside Ye Olde Crown Hotel, pass beneath the railway overbridge and turn left into the car park, continuing to the cycle hire centre at the top end.

Why do this cycle ride?

The scenery of the Hamps and Manifold valleys should be enough to tempt anyone on to this trail which follows the trackbed of a former narrow gauge railway through limestone gorges, and passing by the tantalising remains of the old railway and the industries it served. The terminus at Hulme End has an excellent Visitor and Interpretative Centre.

Researched and written by: Neil Coates

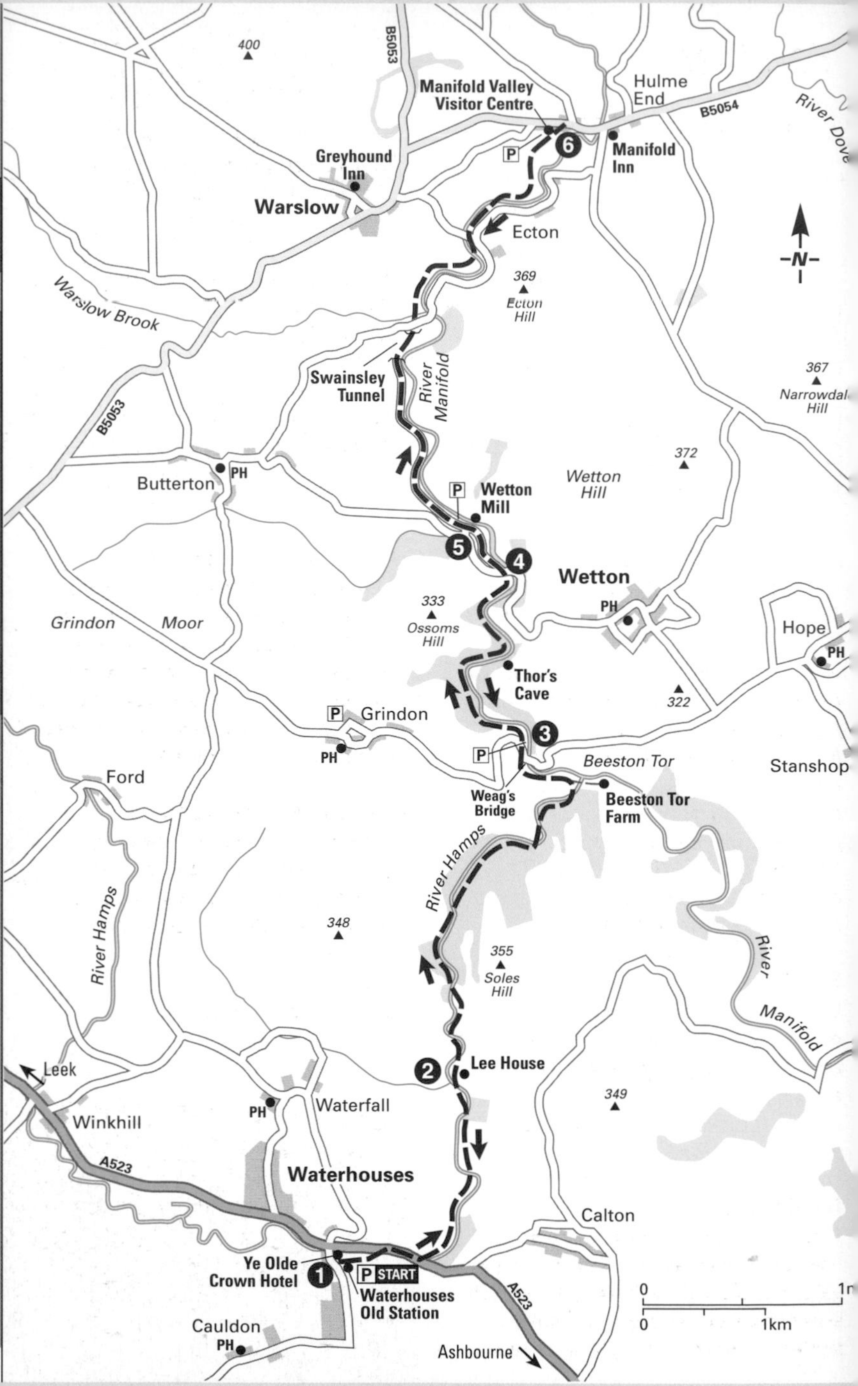

400 ▲

B5053

Manifold Valley
Visitor Centre

Hulme
End

B5054

River Dove

Greyhound
Inn

P   6   Manifold
Inn

Warslow

Ecton

369 ▲
Ecton
Hill

367 ▲
Narrowdal
Hill

Warslow Brook

River Manifold

Swainsley
Tunnel

B5053

Butterton   PH

P   Wetton
Mill

Wetton
Hill

372 ▲

5

4   Wetton

Grindon   Moor

333 ▲
Ossoms
Hill

Thor's
Cave

PH

Hope

PH

322 ▲

Ford

P   Grindon

PH

P

3

Beeston Tor

Stanshop

Weag's
Bridge

Beeston Tor
Farm

River Hamps

River Manifold

348 ▲

355 ▲
Soles
Hill

Leek

2   Lee House

Winkhill

PH

Waterfall

349 ▲

A523

Waterhouses

Calton

Ye Olde
Crown Hotel

1   P START
Waterhouses
Old Station

A523

0   1r
0   1km

Cauldon   PH

Ashbourne

Ye Olde Crown Hotel

about the pub

Ye Olde Crown Hotel
Waterhouses, Stoke-on-Trent
Staffordshire ST10 3HL
Tel 01538 308204

DIRECTIONS:	see Getting to the start
PARKING:	20
OPEN:	daily
FOOD:	daily
BREWERY/COMPANY:	free house
REAL ALE:	Tetley, Burton Ale
ROOMS:	7 bedrooms

12

CYCLE

Manifold   STAFFORDSHIRE

A traditional village local on the banks of the River Hamps, Ye Olde Crown dates from around 1648 when it was built as a coaching inn. Inside are two bars, each sporting original stonework and solid beams, the latter adorned with old water jugs. Log fires are lit in cooler weather. The lounge bar with its Edwardian darkwood half-panelled walls, wall benches and a vast array of copper and brass pieces, provides a comfortable retreat for a traditional pub meal and a pint of Tetleys after a good walk. Homely accommodation includes an adjacent cottage.

Food
Offering a traditional range of pub food, dishes are freshly prepared and take in cod and chips, steak and kidney pie, ham, egg and chips and home-made curries. Daily dishes may include cottage pie, chicken and ham pasta and a good roast lunch.

Family facilities
Families will find a friendly welcome towards children who have their own good-value menu to choose from. Unfortunately, summer alfresco seating and eating is limited to a few tables by the car park.

Alternative refreshment stops
There are tea rooms at Lee House Farm and Wetton Mill along the route. The Yew Tree pub at Cauldon, just 1 mile (1.6km) from the cycle hire centre and along the same road, has a remarkable collection of polyphons, automatic pianos and curios, a great favourite with children.

☛ Where to go from here
The Churnet Valley Railway, based at Cheddleton near Leek, operates steam trains into the beautiful Churnet Valley (www.churnet-valley-railway.co.uk).

Thor's Cave in the Manifold Valley

The Charm of the Churnet

CYCLE

Churnet Valley

STAFFORDSHIRE

Alton Castle, a Victorian building on the site of a Norman castle

Oakamoor. It had been the site of an iron-processing centre for centuries before the industry really found its feet in the 19th century when Thomas Patten & Co developed tinplating and later copper wire foundries here. The copper came from the Duke of Sutherland's mines at Ecton, in the Manifold Valley, and was brought the short distance across the moors by packhorses. Most famously, the copper wire used in the first transatlantic telegraph cable was drawn out here before being laid across the ocean from Isambard Kingdom Brunel's *Great Eastern* steamship.

Trace the route of an old canal and railway to the fascinating industrial village of Oakamoor.

Churnet Valley

Here and there along the way are the scant remains of the former Uttoxeter branch of the Caldon Canal. This 13-mile (20.9km) stretch was built during the early 19th century, running from the canal terminus at the vast limestone works at Froghall through to the market town of Uttoxeter, thereby connecting the town to the main canal network at Stoke-on-Trent. It lasted just 34 years before the North Staffordshire Railway bought out the canal company and built its new line along the Churnet Valley, filling in much of the canal to use as a trackbed.

One impetus for both the canal and railway was the industrial complex at

the ride

1 The route follows the trackbed of the former Churnet Valley Railway which closed in 1965. It starts at a gateway just beyond the village petrol station. Join the old line here, immediately passing between the old platforms. Once past these, the way becomes a grassy trail, with just a narrow strip of compacted gravel offering a surfaced route through the greensward. This is true of the route for the first couple of miles as it forges a way remote from any road or building. At one point it crosses the **River Churnet** and comes close to a muddy, overgrown cut, the first sign of the old canal that the railway replaced in the 1840s. The narrow track widens here and there, eventually becoming more graded as it approaches the village of **Alton**.

2 Keep an eye out for imposing **Alton Castle**. This is Victorian, built on the site of an original Norman castle by the 16th Earl of Shrewsbury and mimics some of the grandiose castles that top crags and hilltops along the Rhine gorge in central Europe. This route doesn't touch the village itself, but sweeps past the stunning old **North Staffordshire Railway (NSR) station**, now a private dwelling.

3 Passing beneath an overbridge, the trackbed runs below sandstone cliffs and beside further marshy stretches of the old canal. The gorge-like quality of the Churnet Valley is best appreciated here before the old line reaches the site of the former station at **Oakamoor**. Keep left of the old platforms here to join an access road that brings the route to the outskirts of the village at the old tunnel keeper's cottage, another striking NSR building. Turn right for the short distance to the village **car park**. It's worth securing your cycles here and following the heritage trail around this fascinating settlement with its surprising history.

4 From the car park here turn left along the lane which, beyond a left fork to join **Red Road**, rises gradually high above the river, then offers an easy passage along this quiet by-road to reach the **Rambler's Retreat** tea rooms and restaurant, a very popular stop for cyclists and walkers

MAP: OS Explorer 259 Derby
START/FINISH: Denstone, grid ref SK 100410
TRAILS/TRACKS: old railway and back lanes
LANDSCAPE: wooded river valley and old villages
PUBLIC TOILETS: none on route
TOURIST INFORMATION: Ashbourne, tel 01335 343666
CYCLE HIRE: none near by
THE PUB: The Bull's Head, High Street, Alton, see Directions to the pub, page 67

Getting to the start
Denstone is on the B5032 about half-way between Cheadle and Ashbourne. In the village follow the signs for Denstone College and park at the village hall or on the roadside near by

Why do this cycle ride?
The Churnet Valley, one of the most peaceful and unspoilt valleys in the Midlands, is dotted with a few small villages but is otherwise remote and picturesque. This easy ride links three of these villages and takes in beautiful wooded sections along the way, encountering surprising industrial heritage and scenery reminiscent of the Rhine Valley in Germany.

Researched and written by: Neil Coates

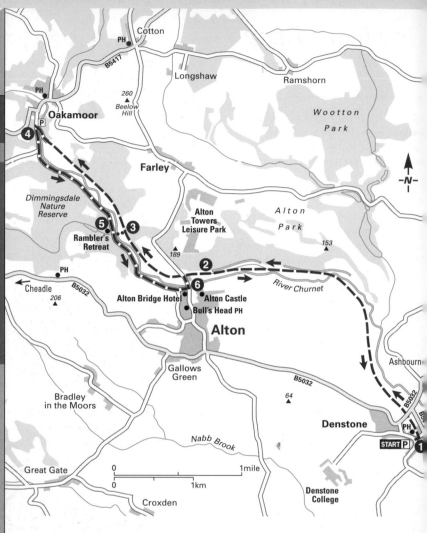

for many years. It's at the edge of the **Dimmingsdale Nature Reserve**, renowned for wild birds and woodland flowers.

5 You have a choice here. To regain the old railway take the gate opposite the car park entrance, cross the **Lord's Bridge** over the river and then the old railway bridge. Immediately left, walk your bike down to the trackbed and turn left beneath the bridge to return to **Denstone**. Alternatively, remain on

Red Road, tracing this along the foot of the gorge to reach the outskirts of **Alton**. Keep left to pass the **Alton Bridge Hotel**.

6 At the main road turn left and cross the river. At the sharp left bend, carefully cross to the right and take the potholed road beside an old factory to find a rough car park and the railway. Keep ahead to return to **Denstone**.

The Bull's Head

about the pub

The Bull's Head
High Street, Alton
Staffordshire ST10 4AQ
Tel 01538 702307
www.thebullsheadinn.co.uk

DIRECTIONS: from Denstone take the B5032 towards Cheadle. At a staggered junction on the edge of Alton take the road signed for Alton Towers. Drop down through the town to a sharp bend where High Street departs straight ahead. The Bull's Head is virtually at this junction

PARKING: 15

OPEN: daily, all day

FOOD: daily

BREWERY/COMPANY: free house

REAL ALE: Bass, Worthington Cask, Greene King, Abbot Ale

ROOMS: 7 bedrooms

Traditional beers, home cooking and well-equipped accommodation are provided at the 300-year-old Bull's Head in the heart of Alton, less than a mile (1.6km) from Alton Towers Leisure Park. Oak beams, impressive wood panelling and an inglenook fireplace set the welcoming scene in the old-world bar, the cosy snug (where children can sit), and the country-style restaurant. Walls, beams and shelves are decorated with a wealth of bric-a-brac ranging from coal scuttles and old stone jars, to candlesticks, brasses and old local photographs. The pub is tucked away amid Georgian and medieval buildings – an area well worth exploring.

Food

Menus offer the likes of sirloin steak, steak and kidney pudding, omelette and chips and deep-fried haddock, alongside filled baguettes and evening specials like chicken and mushroom balti.

Family facilities

Families are made most welcome here; children can settle and relax in the snug bar where they have their own menu to choose from. Outdoor seating is limited to a few tables and chairs on a paved area by the car park.

Alternative refreshment stops

There are pubs in Oakamoor, Alton and Denstone. The Rambler's Retreat restaurant and café is on the route.

☞ Where to go from here

Visit Alton Towers Leisure Park (www.altontowers.com), or Sudbury Hall and Museum of Childhood, to the south east (www.nationaltrust.org).

The Staffordshire Moorlands

CYCLE

A lovely, undulating, on-road route through
the countryside where the White Peak meets
the Dark Peak, visiting Longnor, 'Cardale'
in the television series *Peak Practice*.

Hulme End STAFFORDSHIRE

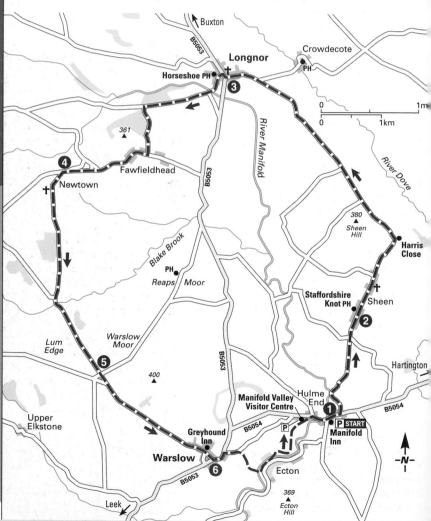

Cycling in the Manifold Valley

Manifold Valley

Before starting out, visit the Manifold Valley Visitor Centre at Hulme End. This is housed in the former village railway station and offers a fascinating glimpse into the history of the area. A series of information boards tell the story of the Manifold Valley, it's remarkable geological heritage and of the light railway that once served this remote community. The canary-yellow carriages and tough little engines last ran in 1934, but a working model in the building helps evoke a sense of place. While you're there, take particular note of the board detailing the heritage to be seen at Ecton, the first station down the line from Hulme End. This is where your return route joins the trackbed of the old railway, and there is much to see including, in summer, rare plants that cling to the spoil tips of the former copper mines, once the most profitable mines in England.

While cycling across the edge of Warslow Moor keep a sharp look out for little owls. They hunt throughout the day and, true to their name, are only about 8in (21cm) high. You may spot one perched on a favourite fencepost, looking for voles or their favourite food – a large beetle.

the ride

1 Take the short steep climb up the B5054 road outside the **Manifold Inn** to a junction on the left signposted '**Sheen & Longnor**'. This winding lane initially descends before starting a gradual climb between limestone walls. Sight lines on

3h30 — 13 MILES — 21 KM — LEVEL 2

MAP: OS Explorer OL24 White Peak
START/FINISH: the Manifold Inn, grid ref SK 108593
TRAILS/TRACKS: all on-road apart from a short section of the Manifold Trail at the end
LANDSCAPE: upland pastures, moorland, limestone gorge
PUBLIC TOILETS: Manifold Valley Visitor Centre, Hulme End; Longnor Market Square
TOURIST INFORMATION: Leek, tel 01538 483741
CYCLE HIRE: Parsley Hay on the High Peak Trail, 4 miles (6.4km) from Hulme End, tel 01298 84493
THE PUB: Manifold Inn, Hulme End, see Point **1** on route
❶ Take care on the short sections of busier road at the start, just beyond Longnor, before Warslow and the very short section of B-road at Warslow. Suitable for older children with on-road cycling experience and not adverse to the odd challenging hill climb

Getting to the start

Hulme End is on the B5054 west of Hartington. Ask at the Manifold Inn if you can park and ride. Alternatively, cross the river bridge and drive to the pay car park at the Manifold Valley Visitor Centre at Hulme End, then cycle to the Manifold Inn.

Why do this cycle ride?

This route rises easily to pleasant back roads across the gritstones of the eastern fringes of the Staffordshire moorlands. The highlight of the route is the little market village of Longnor. The final section is a descent into the Manifold Valley.

Researched and written by: Neil Coates

this section are not good, but they improve after a slightly steeper pitch brings the route to the straggling village of **Sheen**.

2 The road undulates through the village, with good views across the walled pastures to the higher Staffordshire moorlands. Passing by the village inn, the **Staffordshire Knot**, and then the little **church**, the way again steepens slightly as it rises through a few bends to level out past **Harris Close Farm**, with **Sheen Hill**'s rugged top drawing the eye left. Down to the right are occasional views into the limestone valley of the young **River Dove** and across to the knolly hills beyond. A long, easy ride follows, cresting to fall down a fairly short, sharp hill with bad sight lines. At the junction keep ahead to reach **Longnor**; from this short section are views across to the hamlet of Crowdecote and up the Dove to the sharp peaks of Chrome and Parkhouse hills.

3 At the heart of Longnor is the **Market Square**. This route crosses straight over the junction here, in front of the **Horseshoe pub** and along a lane signposted '**Royal Cottage and Leek**'. Once out of the village there's a steep descent to a bridge over the **River Manifold**, heralding the start of a long steady climb up the valley side. On the right is the imposing old village **sawmill**, being transformed into apartments. In 0.5 mile (800m) the route levels along a long tree-lined straight to reach a left turn signposted '**Fawfieldhead and Newtown**'. Follow this through to a T-junction and

turn right along a pleasant undulating lane with pleasing views.

4 At a telephone box turn left along a lane signposted '**Warslow**'. Soon you'll pass by the little **chapel** at **Newtown** (built 1837) off to your right in its overgrown churchyard. This is an airy, easy cruise along a high road, with the distinctive limestone hills at Ecton the main feature off to your left beyond **Reaps Moor**. Beyond a house called Hayshead the lane starts a long, gradual climb before levelling out beside **Lum Edge** and **Warslow Moor**.

5 Go straight across the crossroads and then bear left at the junction, joining a quite well-used road that rises gradually, soon crossing a cattle grid. Cresting another rise, there's a long, sweeping descent into **Warslow**, passing the **Greyhound Inn** to reach a junction with the B5053.

6 Turn left along this road and remain on it for about 200yds (183m) to find a lane on the right, signposted 'Unsuitable for Heavy Goods Vehicles'. Carefully turn into this, which drops increasingly steeply as a narrow, winding lane. Keep right to descend to a bridge across the **Manifold**. Just beyond this turn left along the **Manifold Way** and follow this to **Hulme End**. Rejoin the main road and turn right to return to the nearby **Manifold Inn**.

A quiet lane that is perfect for cyclists near the Manifold Railway Visitor Centre

Manifold Inn

about the pub

Manifold Inn
Hulme End, Hartington
Buxton, Derbyshire SK17 0EX
Tel 01298 84537
www.themanifoldinn.co.uk

DIRECTIONS: see Getting to the start
PARKING: 25
OPEN: daily, all day Saturday and Sunday
May–September
FOOD: daily
BREWERY/COMPANY: free house
REAL ALE: Black Sheep Special, Hartington
Arbor Light, Boddington's, guest beer
ROOMS: 7 en suite

Standing beside a bridge over the River Manifold and sheltered by a stand of pines, the Manifold Inn is a lovely, imposing, gabled stone building, originally built as a coaching inn some 200 years ago. Its fortunes were rejuvenated when the Leek and Manifold Light Railway opened in 1904 and it changed its name to The Light Railway Hotel, a name it retained until 1984 (50 years after the line closed). Inside, the only public room is comfortable and well presented – a solid wood bar fronts a carpeted room with plenty of beams, horse brasses, old photos and paintings of the pub, with a large wood-burning stove taking pride of place.

Food

The ever-changing chalkboard menu may list home-made soups or chicken liver pâté for starters, with mains ranging from haddock, chips and mushy peas, and lasagne to lamb shank with minted *jus*,
beef Wellington and grilled lemon sole. There are lighter snacks at lunchtime.

Family facilities

Children are welcome away from the bar. Although there are no special facilities or menu (smaller portions are available), the place is very popular with families. The good summer garden is shaded by mature trees.

Alternative refreshment stops

There are pubs on the route at Sheen (Staffordshire Knot), Longnor (4 pubs) and Warslow (the Greyhound Inn). Cafés and tea rooms at Longnor.

☛ Where to go from here

Blackbrook Zoological Park (at Winkhill, south west of Hulme End, off the A523) is a rare breeds centre specialising in birds, but with some mammals, reptiles, tropical fish and a children's petting corner (www.blackbrookzoologicalpark.co.uk).

Pennine Ways on Kinder Scout

WALK

The Pennine Way

DERBYSHIRE

One end of the famous long distance trail ascends to the craggy outcrops of the Kinder Plateau.

The Pennine Way

Edale sits peacefully in a paradise of pasture, riverside meadow and hedgerow, surrounded by high peaks, the crags of Kinder Scout, and the rounded hills of the Mam Tor ridge.

In Depression-torn 1930s England, Tom Stephenson, then secretary of the Ramblers' Association told the readers of the *Daily Herald* of his dream to create a long, green trail across the roof of England. It took 30 years, a mass trespass and Acts of Parliament to achieve, but in 1965, the Pennine Way was opened. Spanning over 250 miles (405km) from Edale to Kirk Yetholm in Scotland it was Britain's first official long distance trail. Go to Edale any Friday night and you'll see eager Pennine Wayfarers poring over Ordnance Survey maps or looking through Wainwright's little green guidebook.

Unfortunately the popularity of the Way has led to the main route through Grindsbrook being diverted along the foul weather route up Jacob's Ladder. But as you leave Edale, or to be more strictly correct Grindsbrook Booth, you can look across to the old route, which delves deep into the rocky ravine. Your route climbs boldly to the top of Ringing Roger (the echoing rocks), with an edge walk round the great chasm of Grindsbrook, taking you past Nether Tor to the place where the old Pennine Way track comes to meet you. The Way didn't bother with the comforts of the edge, but got stuck into those peat hags to the right. Past

weather-smoothed gritstone sculptures and the rocky peak of Grindslow Knoll you come to another ravine – Crowden Brook.

This route descends by the brook, passing several waterfalls. Beneath the open fell the path seeks the recently planted pine, larch, birch and oak. Wild flowers, including bluebells, daffodils and primroses, proliferate in this delightful spot, just above Upper Booth. Finally you meet again the Pennine Way, following the new route back across the fields of Edale.

the walk

1 Turn right out of the car park pedestrian entrance beside the toilet block and head north into **Edale** village, under the railway and past the **Old Nags Head**. Turn right by a path sign and follow the path across the footbridge over **Grinds Brook**.

2 Leave the main **Grindsbrook Clough** path by the side of a barn, taking the right fork that climbs up the lower hillslope

Left : A stone path at the start of the Pennine Way
Below right: Walking on the Pennine Way

to a gate on the edge of open country. Beyond the gate the path zig-zags above **Fred Herdman's Plantation** then climbs up the nose of the Nab to the skyline rocks. Where the path divides, take the right fork to the summit rocks of **Ringing Roger**.

3 Head towards the edge, left of a hut, climbing a few rough steps to gain the path along the rim of the plateau. For a long way it is paved. Follow this path above the cavernous hollow of **Grindsbrook** and past **Nether Tor**. The old **Pennine Way** route is met on the east side by a large cairn.

4 Ignoring the left fork heading for the outlier of **Grindslow Knoll**, follow the paved footpath right (west) to the head of another deep hollow, the clough of **Crowden Brook**.

5 Cross Crowden Brook, then immediately leave the edge to follow a narrow level path traversing slopes on the left beneath the imposing outcrop of **Crowden Tower**. This meets a rough path from the Tower before descending the steep grassy hillslopes to the banks of the brook. This is a very steep, rough descent and requires

MAP: OS Explorer OL1 Dark Peak
START/FINISH: Edale pay car park; grid ref SK 125853
PATHS: rock and peat paths, about 16 stiles and gates
LANDSCAPE: heather moor
PUBLIC TOILETS: at car park
TOURIST INFORMATION: Edale, tel 01433 670207
THE PUB: The Old Nags Head, Hope Valley, see Point **1** on route

⚠ There is a long, steep climb near the start of this walk. The return from Crowden Tower is particularly steep and potentially slippery. Recommended for experienced family walking groups only

Getting to the start
From Sheffield take the A625 and follow the brown tourist signs for the caverns at Castleton. At Hope, turn right for Edale opposite the church; in 5 miles (8km) turn right into the car park at Edale. Edale Station is served by trains on the Sheffield to Manchester line.

Researched and written by:
Neil Coates, John Gillham

what to look for
You walk along the edge of Kinder Scout's summit peat bogs. Peat was formed by mosses such as the bright green sphagnum moss you'll see on wet patches. The moss cover is now restricted to small patches. It has been replaced by sedges, grasses, heather and bilberry in a vegetation cover riven by deep and numerous hags in which the naked peat comes to the surface.

great care. The path now follows the brook, fording it on several occasions.

6 Go through the stile at the edge of open country, then cross a footbridge shaded by tall rowans to change to the west bank. From here the path threads through woodland before descending in steps to the road at **Upper Booth**. You now need to follow the **Pennine Way** path back to **Edale**.

7 Turn left along the lane and left again into Upper Booth farmyard before crossing a stile at the top right corner, signposted for Edale. After following a track to a gateway, bear left uphill to a stile above an old barn. Here the way traverses fields at the foot of **Broadlee Bank** before joining a tree-lined track into the village at the Old Nags Head. Turn right down the road back to the car park.

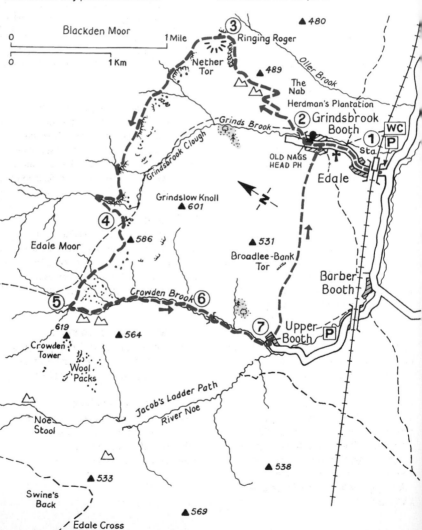

Old Nags Head

about the pub

The Old Nags Head
Hope Valley, Edale
Derbyshire S33 7ZA
Tel 01433 670291

DIRECTIONS: see Getting to the start	
PARKING: 10	
OPEN: all day, closed Monday and Tuesday November–Easter	
BAR MEALS: daily, all day Saturday and Sunday	
BREWERY/COMPANY: free house	
REAL ALE: Grays Best and Premium, guest beer	
DOGS: welcome throughout the pub (drinking bowls)	

The Old Nags Head, one of the most renowned ramblers' pubs in the land, stands at the start (or end!) of the Pennine Way National Trail, England's classic 256-mile (412km) long distance footpath. Its setting is dramatic, with the great scalloped edges of Kinder Scout looming above the sandstone tiles and its long, low gritstone façade broken by a couple of gables overlooking the village square. Climbing roses scale the front, whilst hanging baskets and raised beds brighten summer days. Booted walkers can choose from a series of flagstone rooms that radiate from the bar in the front room. The Hiker's Bar has an open log fire – great for warming the toes on cold days. This is a welcome retreat offering good beer and wholesome pub food.

Food
On the basic pub menu you'll find the Nags Head Special, a giant Yorkshire pudding filled with beef stew; steak, ale and mushroom pie; leek and potato bake, and a good range of sandwiches and filled jacket potatoes. Chalkboard offerings may include mushroom and nut fettucini.

Family facilities
To the rear of the pub (and with its own access) there is a popular family room. Here children have their own menu to choose from, while on warmer days they can use the front terrace or the garden and enjoy the views.

Alternative refreshment stops
The Rambler Inn, also in Edale, serves good bar meals and there's a snack bar in an old railway carriage by the railway station.

☛ Where to go from here
Peak Cavern, in nearby Castleton, offers tours of the cave and demonstrations of the old craft of ropemaking (www.peakcavern.co.uk).

Mam Tor and Rushup Edge

Mam Tor

DERBYSHIRE

Approaching from the Edale side, discover the ancient secrets of the great 'Shivering Mountain'.

The 'Shivering Mountain'

With its spectacular views and close proximity to the road it's hardly surprising that Mam Tor is the most popular of the Peak District hill forts. Unfortunately this popularity has resulted in the National Trust having to pave the footpath and a large area around the summit to prevent serious erosion.

Called the Shivering Mountain because of the instability of its shale layers, Mam Tor is the largest of the Peak's hill forts and has the distinction of being the only one to be excavated. In the mid-1960s Manchester University selected Mam Tor as a training site for its archaeology students and this produced a wealth of fresh information about the fort. What can be seen today are the ramparts of a heavily fortified Iron-Age settlement. The single rampart with an outer ditch and another bank can still be traced round the hillside. There were two entrances, one leading to the path from Hollins Cross and the other to the path

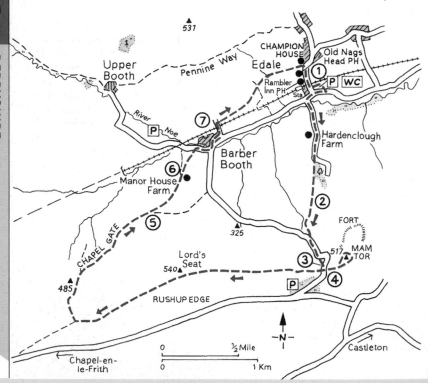

to Mam Nick. Mam Tor was probably a partially defended site with a timber palisade that was later replaced with stone.

The excavations revealed that there had been a settlement here long before the Iron Age. Two Early Bronze-Age barrows were discovered on the summit, one of which the National Trust has capped in stone to make sure it is preserved. An earlier settlement on the ground enclosed by the ramparts was excavated. Here several circular houses or huts had been built on terraced platforms on the upper slopes of the hill. The pottery and other artefacts uncovered are of a style often found in house platforms of this type and date from the Late Bronze Age. Radiocarbon dating of charcoal found in the huts put them somewhere between 1700 and 1000 BC.

Archaeologists, GDB Jones and FH Thomson, writing about the discoveries at Mam Tor, suggested that the fort might have been built as a shelter for pastoralists using the hills for summer grazing, but decided in the end that it was more likely to have had a strategic military purpose. Depending on when it was actually built, it could have seen action during inter-tribal struggles of the native Brigantes. It may well at a later period have been used as a strategic defence against the advancing Romans. Like most settlements from this far back in time Mam Tor will probably never reveal all its secrets, but standing on the summit and looking away down the valleys on either side, back along the path to Hollins Cross or forward to Rushup Edge it's enough just to try and imagine the effort that went into building such an enormous fortification with nothing but the most primitive of tools.

3h30 — 6 MILES — 9.7 KM — LEVEL 2

WALK

MAP: OS Explorer OL1 Dark Peak
START/FINISH: good public car park at Edale, grid ref SK 124853
PATHS: mainly good but can be boggy in wet weather, 15 stiles and gates
LANDSCAPE: woodland, hills and meadows
PUBLIC TOILETS: at car park
TOURIST INFORMATION: Edale, tel 01433 670207
THE PUB: The Rambler Inn, Hope Valley, near the start of the walk

🅛 To be tackled by older, fitter children. There is a long and fairly arduous stretch near the start of this route

Getting to the start

From Sheffield take the A625 and follow the brown tourist signs for the caverns at Castleton. At Hope, turn right for Edale opposite the church; in 5 miles (8km) turn right into the main car park at Edale. The adjoining Edale Station is served by regular trains on the Sheffield to Manchester line.

Researched and written by:
Neil Coates, Moira McCrossan, Hugh Taylor

Mam Tor

DERBYSHIRE

Mam Tor

DERBYSHIRE

the walk

1 Exit the car park entrance at **Edale** and turn right on to the road past a phone box. In 200yds (183m) turn left along a farm road for Hardenclough Farm. Just before this road turns sharply left take the public footpath that forks off to the right and goes uphill through a wood.

2 At the end of the wooded area cross a stile and continue uphill. Cross another stile, follow the path across open hillside, then cross yet another stile and turn left on to the road. Just before the road bends sharply left, cross the road, go over a stile and follow this path towards a hill.

3 Near the foot of the hill cross the stile to the left and turn right on to the road. Continue to find the steps on the left leading through the ramparts of an Iron-Age fort to the summit of **Mam Tor**. From here retrace your steps back to the road.

4 Cross the road, go over a stile and continue on the footpath uphill and on to **Rushup Edge**. Follow this well-defined path along the ridge crossing five stiles. When the path is intersected by another, go right. This is **Chapel Gate** track, badly eroded by off-road motorbikes. Go through a kissing gate then head downhill.

5 Near the bottom of the hill go through a gap stile on the left. Go through another stile, join a raised path and go through a handgate, then cross another stile on the left. This leads to some tumbledown buildings. Cross over a stile by the corner of one building then veer right and cross another stile on to a rough farm road.

6 Cross this diagonally and follow the path beside a brook. Cross this and walk through to a lane. Turn right, then left at the junction. Cross the bridge and fork ahead on to the lane through the hamlet of **Barber Booth**. Near the far end fork left up a gated, rough lane signposted for Edale Station.

7 Follow the path across a series of meadows, going through several gates and stiles to join the road to Edale Station next to **Champion House**. Turn right on to the road then, near the junction, turn left into the car park.

what to look for

Look out over Edale from Rushup Edge to Kinder Scout, scene of a mass trespass by ramblers in 1932. They were exercising what they saw to be their right to roam the hills and moors. Several were jailed and the severity of their sentences made them martyrs and heroes. Many people today believe that this act is what led ultimately to the creation of national parks.

Top: A view over the Peak District from Mam Tor

The Rambler Inn

The Rambler is a thriving pub which welcomes walkers, cyclists and the countless day visitors that descend on this beautiful area. Built of honey-coloured gritstone, with gables and large windows, it stands in its own grounds at the bottom of Edale's one village road. From the lawned gardens, with mature trees, there are stunning views down the valley of the River Noe. Inside, three airy rooms have high ceilings, reflecting the Rambler's Victorian origins, and a mix of flagstone, quarry tiled and carpeted floors. The comfortable furnishings consist of a mix of lived-in old wing armchairs, wooden seats and chairs and a mish-mash of tables. Blazing winter log fires in each room draw weary walkers in for Grays ales and traditional pub food.

about the pub

The Rambler Inn
Hope Valley, Edale
Derbyshire S33 7ZA
Tel 01433 670268.
www.theramblerinn.co.uk

DIRECTIONS: next to Edale Station and near the main village car park– see Getting to the start

PARKING: 20

OPEN: daily, all day

FOOD: all day

BREWERY/COMPANY: free house

REAL ALE: Grays Best, Premium and L S Lowry Bitter, guest beer

DOGS: on a lead in the bar only

ROOMS: 9 bedrooms

Food
The menus offer traditional pub food ranging from large ploughman's lunches, sandwiches and basic pub snacks, to lamb chops, chips and peas, haddock and chips, and a mammoth Ramblers' Grill.

Family facilities
Children are welcome in the pub away from the bar area and can choose from a standard children's menu. On sunny summer days they can enjoy the spacious gardens and let off steam in the large activity playground.

Alternative refreshment stops
Café near Edale Station, also Old Nags Head pub in Edale (see page 75)

☞ Where to go from here
Treak Cliff Cavern in Castleton is the main source of the famous Blue John stone, unique to this Derbyshire village (www.bluejohnstone.com).

The White Peak Plateau

CYCLE

From the High Peak Trail and excellent by-roads to timeless villages and old churches.

Ancient Walls

One of the great characteristics of the White Peak are the miles of dry-stone walls that thread the landscape from valley bottom to the very tops of the plateau. You can pass them by without giving them a second thought, but they have a fascinating history that goes back to medieval times when the great monastic estates controlled huge tracts of land and boundaries were established between these religious holdings and the lands of the great families.

As the monasteries disappeared, their lands were gradually parcelled up, and a further phase of wall building occurred. These walls are often winding and uneven. Huge areas still remained open however. As well as the wealthy estates, poor villagers also were permitted to farm dispersed strips of land near their homes. These initially were separated by low earth embankments. From the early 1700s onwards land reform saw such holdings consolidated into larger areas, each separated by a stone wall. These small strip fields can be seen at Chelmorton.

The Enclosure Awards of, largely, the 18th century, saw the great, unwalled estates split up into regular 'Parliamentary' fields (each Enclosure Award needed an Act of Parliament); it is these regular, geometric walls that form the mosaic that dominate today's landscape. Some walls were even built by French prisoners during the Napoleonic Wars.

the ride

1 Ride north along the old railway, leaving the **Royal Oak** on your left. The current end of the High Peak Trail at **Dowlow** is soon reached; turn right here along a surfaced track for **Chee Dale** that heads for the A515. This is marked on the OS map as a footpath, but has been upgraded as part of the development of the **Pennine Bridleway** project and is open to pedal cycles. A fenced path beside the A515 then takes you right to a crossing point. Take great care crossing directly over here and join a lane heading north.

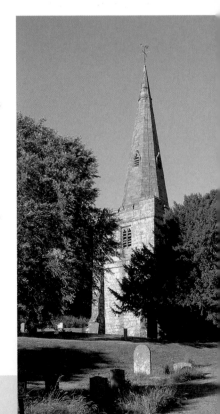

2 This peaceful lane undulates across the limestone uplands, with grand vistas all around across a patchwork of old stone walls and hay meadows. Where the **Pennine Bridleway** joins a rough lane, you remain on the tarred road. A lengthy downhill freewheel brings you to a crossroads. Carefully cross straight over and continue along the lane, rising very gradually up the one street that makes up **Chelmorton**. Continue to the end to find the old **church**.

3 Drop back downhill again slightly to reach a left turn; take this and start a lengthy but shallow climb back up on to the breezy uplands. At the T-junction turn left, signposted **'Flagg and Taddington'**, joining a largely flat road with excellent sight lines. Again, there are great views and there is little traffic to disturb your enjoyment. At the next junction turn right, signed **Flagg**, starting a good long descent into the village. Keep left at a bend, dropping along the straggling main street of the village and past the little **church**. Keep left to arrive at the **Plough Inn**, at the edge of the village.

4 Continue past the Plough for about 500yds (457m) to a right turn for **Monyash**, joining a rather bumpy surfaced lane and soon a long, easy descent to a T-junction. Here turn right, signed Monyash, to another long downhill cruise to the outskirts of **Monyash**. A short climb brings you to the village centre crossroads, village green and the **Bull's Head Inn**.

The small church at Chelmorton

4h00 — **11.5 MILES** — **18.4 KM** — **LEVEL 2**

MAP: OS Explorer OL24 White Peak
START/FINISH POINT: Hurdlow car park, High Peak Trail, grid ref SK 128660
TRAILS/TRACKS: old railway track, back lanes with light traffic
LANDSCAPE: small walled fields, views across the White Peak plateau
PUBLIC TOILETS: Parsley Hay
TOURIST INFORMATION: Buxton, tel 01298 25106
CYCLE HIRE: Parsley Hay 01298 84493, www.derbyshire.gov.uk/countryside
THE PUB: The Plough Inn, Main Street, Flagg, see Point 4 on route

🛈 Two direct crossings of an A road need care. Suitable for older children and/or fitter cyclists, one long climb of around 0.5 miles (800m) requires regular rest stops

Getting to the start
Hurdlow car park (named Sparklow on OS maps) on the High Peak Trail, is signposted off the A515 Buxton to Ashbourne road about 6 miles (9.7km) south of Buxton. At the crossroads signed for Monyash in one direction and Crowdecote/Longnor in the other, turn towards Longnor to the car park

Why do this cycle ride?
This is an easy, flowing route along quiet back roads and a section of the Pennine Bridleway. Largely level, quiet, minor roads skim between walled fields to charming villages. Rising gently to Monyash, lanes then rise steeply to the White Peak plateau before an exhilarating ride back to the start.

Researched and written by: Neil Coates

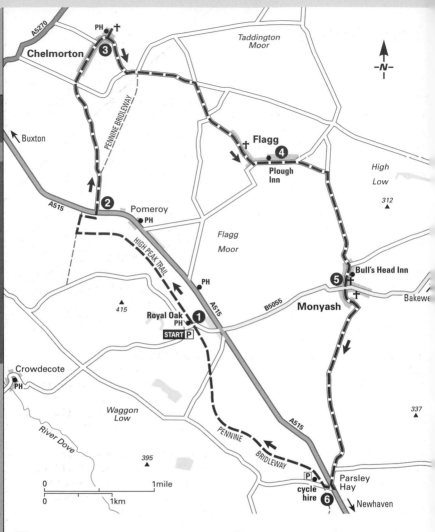

5 Carefully cross directly over, taking **Rakes Road**, signposted '**Newhaven and Youlgreave**' and continue with a long ascent out of Monyash. Allow plenty of time to pause and take in the superb panorama across the southern stretches of the Peak District, easily visible over the low limestone walls. The road gradually levels out before dropping to the A515.

6 Take care crossing here, as the traffic can be fast despite restrictions on both speed and overtaking here. Go diagonally across to the lane signposted for the **Parsley Hay car park**. Just along the lane turn right along the access road to the car park. Pick up the **High Peak Trail** here and follow it north (signed as the Pennine Bridleway towards Peak Forest) to return to the car park at Hurdlow.

The Plough Inn

Flagg is no more than a strand of roadside farms and cottages surrounded by pastures, hay meadows and cornfields, so it's good to find that the pub in this secluded hamlet is thriving. Set well back from the lane, the Plough is a solid limestone building with a warren of little rooms radiating off the main bar room which features a splendid log fire, heavy beams, a few window seats and old local photos on the walls. Off to one end is a large pool and games room; at the other end is a light and airy luncheon room with light-blue walls, wicker-style chairs and pub dining tables. Upstairs there is a superb little restaurant, open to the rafters with an air of the East and a faint touch of Gothic decoration. An excellent pub, well worth passing the others on the route to find.

Food

You'll find an extensive printed bar menu offering Lancashire hotpot, lasagne, salmon en croute, steak and kidney pudding, a good range of steaks and a chalkboard listing several daily specials. The same menu serves the upstairs restaurant.

about the pub

The Plough Inn
Main Street, Flagg, Buxton
Derbyshire SK17 9QR
Tel 01298 85557

DIRECTIONS: the pub is on the route; alternatively it can be reached by following signs off the A515 south east of Buxton
PARKING: 40
OPEN: daily, all day Saturday and Sunday. Closed Monday lunchtime
FOOD: daily
BREWERY/COMPANY: free house
REAL ALE: Timothy Taylor Landlord, Marston's Pedigree, guest beers
ROOMS: 2 en suite

Family facilities

In summer, families should head for the hedged and lawned beer garden which enjoys rurals views. Children are most welcome indoors and youngsters have their own menu to choose from.

Alternative refreshment stops

There are pubs at Sparklow (Royal Oak), Chelmorton (Church Inn) and Monyash (The New Inn); tea rooms in Monyash; snacks at Parsley Hay.

☛ Where to go from here

Buxton Spa Water is freely available from an ever-flowing tap in St Ann's Terrace, on The Crescent. On the southern edge of Buxton is Poole's Cavern, where you'll find Derbyshire's largest stalactite (www.poolescavern.co.uk).

Pilsbury Castle and the Upper Dove Valley

The upper valley of the Dove is one of quiet villages and historic remains.

Hartington and Pilsbury Castle

Hartington, lying in the mid-regions of the Dove Valley, is a prosperous village with fine 18th-century houses and hotels built in local limestone and lined around spacious greens. The settlement's history can be traced back to the Normans, when it was recorded as Hartedun, the centre for the De Ferrier's estate. Hartington Hall, now the youth hostel, was first built in 1350 but was substantially rebuilt in 1611.

As you leave the village, the lane climbs past the church of St Giles, which has a splendid battlemented Perpendicular tower. It continues up the high valley sides of the Dove and on through an emerald landscape of high fields and valley.

Pilsbury Castle hides until the last moment, but then a grassy ramp swoops down to it from the hillsides. Only the earthworks are now visible, but you can imagine its impregnable position on a limestone knoll that juts out into the valley. You can see the motte, a man-made mound built to accommodate the wooden keep, and the bailey, a raised embankment that would have had a wooden stockade round it. The castle's exact history is disputed. It was probably built around 1100 by the Normans, on the site of an Iron-Age fort. It may have been a stronghold used earlier by William I to suppress a local rebellion in his 'Wasting of the North' campaign. Being in the middle of the De Ferrier estate it was probably their administrative centre. In the

what to look for

The Dairy Crest Creamery is one of only a few places which are licensed to make Stilton Cheese. There's a visitor centre in Hartington, where you can sample and buy. Look too for Hartington Hall, an impressive three-gabled manor house, now the youth hostel (see photo).

1200s this function would have been moved to Hartington.

Views up-valley are fascinating with the conical limestone peaks of Parkhouse and Chrome Hills in the distance. Now the route descends into Dovedale for the first time, crossing the river into Staffordshire. The lane climbs to a high lane running the length of the dale's east rim. Note the change in the rock – it's now the darker gritstone. The crags of Sheen Hill have been blocking the view east, but once past them you can see for miles, across the Manifold Valley to the Roaches and Hen Cloud. A field path takes the route on its finale, descending along a line of crags with lofty views of Hartington and the end of the walk.

the walk

1 Turn left out of the car park and follow the lane to the right beside the village green. Turn left up **Hide Lane** by the **church** and take the second path on the left in 600yds (549m), just past a large modern barn. This heads northwards across fields. Below a farm complex, the path swings left to follow a dry-stone wall on the left.

2 The path cuts down the concrete drive coming up the hill from **Bank Top Farm**. Waymarking posts highlight the continuing route along the high valley sides, about 50yds (45m) up from the break of slope.

Hartington Hall dates from 1611 and is now a youth hostel

3h30 · **7.5 MILES** · **12.1 KM** · **LEVEL 1 2**

MAP: OS Explorer OL24 White Peak

START/FINISH: Hartington pay car park, grid ref SK 127603

PATHS: field paths and lanes, some steep climbs, about 32 stiles and gates

LANDSCAPE: pastures, limestone valley

PUBLIC TOILETS: at car park

TOURIST INFORMATION: Ashbourne, tel 01335 343666

THE PUB: The Packhorse Inn, Crowdecote, see Point **5** on route

⓵ This is a long walk with several ascents and is best suited to older children

Getting to the start

From Buxton take the A515 south towards Ashbourne. Pass the Jug and Glass Inn and then look for the right turn on the B5054 for Hartington.

Researched and written by: Neil Coates, John Gillham

3 West of **Carder Low** (grid ref 126627) the path goes through a gateway by an intersection of walls and becomes indistinct. Here, climb half right to another gateway, then head for a group of trees. Below these another footpath signpost shows the way uphill and half right to a step stile in a ridge wall, where you look down into a small valley.

4 Descend into the valley and turn left at a fingerpost for **Pilsbury** and Crowdecote to reach a lane by a stone barn. A stile across the road allows you on to the continuing path, rounding the high slopes above Pilsbury. The footpath rakes left down the hill slopes to a farm track and wall alongside the ancient earthworks of **Pilsbury Castle**. Go through the stile here.

5 Turn right along the path, which takes a well-used course heading up the valley, gradually losing height to join the valley floor. Cross straight over a rough, walled field track. The path develops into a farm track; remain with this past **Bridge End Farm** to reach **Crowdecote** and the **Packhorse Inn**.

6 Retrace your steps to Bridge End Farm. Beside the barn look right for a footbridge across the **Dove** (there's a hidden fingerpost, left). Walk ahead up the field.

7 The path steepens up the valley side. After a walker's gate veer right, away from the wall, climbing up through scrub to reach the Longnor road. Turn left along the lane to reach **Harris Close Farm** in 2 miles (3.2km).

Right: The hamlet of Pilsbury
Page 87: The mound of Pilsbury Castle

8 Turn into the drive and look immediately on the right for a narrow passage right of the low barn. This leads to a fieldside path. In all but one field there's a wall on the right for guidance. After going through a wood, in 50yds (45m) the path descends through scrub into the valley. It joins a farm track southwards towards **Bridge End Farm**.

9 At the fingerpost for **Hartington**, turn left through a gate and cross a field. Cross the **Dove** by a footbridge hidden by trees. The path gradually swings right (south east) across fields, aims for the woods to the left of the dairy and enters them via a stile. At the other side go into the forecourt of the dairy and turn left along the lane to return to **Hartington**.

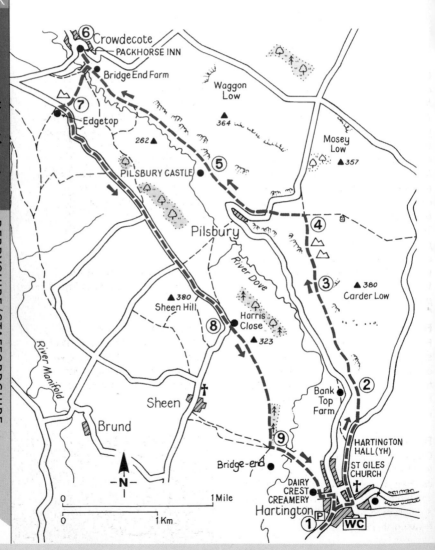

The Packhorse Inn

about the pub

The Packhorse Inn
Crowdecote, Buxton
Derbyshire SK17 0DB
Tel 01298 83618

DIRECTIONS: on Point 5 of the route, see Getting to the start, in the centre of Crowdecote off the A515 north west of Hartington

PARKING: 20

OPEN: all day Saturday and Sunday, Easter to September. Closed Monday, except Bank Holidays when it closes on Tuesday instead

FOOD: daily

BREWERY/COMPANY: free house

REAL ALE: Worthington Cask, Timothy Taylor Landlord, guest beer

DOGS: welcome throughout pub

ROOMS: 2 bedrooms

Crowdecote consists of a huddle of cottages and farms clinging to a steep hillside above the juvenile River Dove. Tucked away in this hamlet is the 300-year-old Packhorse Inn, once frequented by trains of packhorses and their overseers, the jaggers. Although the little interconnecting rooms have been updated over the years they retain some of their original character, with solid beams, stone walls and open fires. With Timothy Taylor Landlord on tap, decent pies and sandwiches on the menu, and a terraced lawn rising up behind with views to the steep slopes of the Dove Valley, this homely, unassuming little pub makes a great halfway stop.

Food

From a weekly changing menu choose starters such as red mullet and cod fishcakes or a bowl of *moules* with crusty bread, or tuck into something more substantial like home-made steak and Guinness pie. There is a good sandwich menu.

Family facilities

On fine sunny days the terraced garden, with the added attractions of ducks and chickens, is the place to be. Inside, children can choose from their own menu, or order a small portion of many of the dishes featured on the main menu.

Alternative refreshment stops

The Charles Cotton Hotel in Hartington (free house)

☛ Where to go from here

Poole's Cavern in Buxton Country Park offers guided tours of the illuminated chambers and their amazing crystal formations (www.poolescavern.co.uk).

Hartington

DERBYSHIRE/STAFFORDSHIRE

Castles and Caverns at Castleton

Castleton is where the limestone of the White Peak and the shales and gritstone of the Dark Peak collide.

Castleton and Cavedale

Castleton, a bustling tourist town, is the last settlement before the Hope Valley narrows and squeezes into the rocky ravine of Winnats. At Castleton the shales and gritstone of the Dark Peak and the limestone plateaux of the White Peak meet. Here countless generations of miners have dug shafts and enlarged the natural caves that riddle the bedrock in search of ore. Here too, they built a road that eventually succumbed to the landslides of Mam Tor, 'the Shivering Mountain'. The castle keep is perched on an outcrop of limestone. It's one of the earliest stone-built castles in the country, built shortly after the Norman

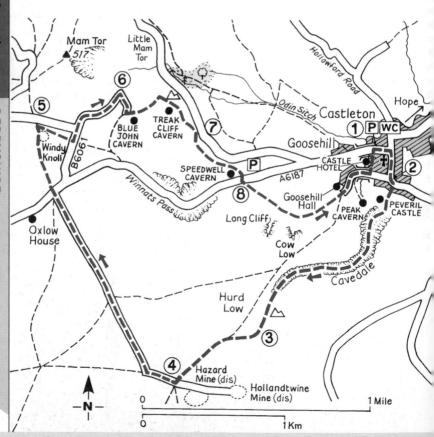

Conquest by William Peveril, William the Conqueror's illegitimate son.

The entrance to Cavedale is narrow and dramatic. From the village square you turn a corner and enter an awesome limestone ravine. Geologists used to think Cavedale was a collapsed cavern, but current thinking places it as a valley carved by glaciers of the last Ice Age. A little limestone path takes you through the ravine, climbing past cave entrances and over the tops of a system of subterranean passages, including those of the nearby Peak Cavern. The valley shallows and the next stretch of the journey is over high green fields enclosed by dry-stone walls. Mam Tor, the Shivering Mountain, dominates the view ahead and soon you look down on the crumbling tarmac of the ill-fated road and huge shale landslides.

The first Castleton cavern of the day is the Blue John Cavern, high on the side of Mam Tor. It takes its name from the purple-blue fluorspar, unique to Castleton. The floodlights of the chambers show off the old river galleries with crystalline waterfalls, and an array of stalagmites and stalactites.

Winnat's Pass winding through the Peak District beyond Castleton

3h00   5 MILES   8 KM   LEVEL 12 3

WALK

MAP: OS Explorer OL1 Dark Peak

START/FINISH: main Castleton pay car park, grid ref SK 149829

PATHS: mostly good limestone paths and old moorland roads, muddy in wet weather; around 16 stiles and gates

LANDSCAPE: limestone ravines and high pastureland

PUBLIC TOILETS: at car park

TOURIST INFORMATION: Castleton, tel 01433 620679

THE PUB: Castle Hotel in the centre of Castleton, set back off the main road

There are some steep slopes towards the end of the walk between the entrances to Blue John and Treak Cliff Caverns. The path below Blue John Cavern can be tricky in wintry conditions

Getting to the start

From Sheffield take the A625 south west and turn right on to the A6187 near Hathersage, following the brown tourist signs for the Caverns at Castleton. The main village car park is through the village on the right.

Researched and written by:
Neil Coates, John Gillham

Castleton

DERBYSHIRE

19

WALK

Castleton

DERBYSHIRE

Beyond the Blue John Cavern, a path crosses the slopes past Treak Cliff Cavern to the Speedwell Cavern, at the foot of Winnats Pass. Here, lead miners excavated a level into the hill, through which they built a subterranean canal, 547yds (500m) long. This took them eleven years, but low yields and high costs forced the early closure of the mine. Take a boat trip down the canal to a landing stage just short of the 'Bottomless Pit', named because the spoil thrown in by miners made no impression on its depth.

The last stretch takes you across the National Trust's Longcliffe Estate. Before retreating to Castleton, take a look back up the valley, and across the limestone that was once a coral reef in a tropical lagoon.

the walk

1 From the car park turn left down the main street, then right along **Castle Street**, passing the **church** and the youth hostel.

2 On reaching the **Market Place**, turn left to **Bar Gate**, where a signpost points to **Cavedale**. Through a gate, the path enters the limestone gorge with the ruined keep of **Peveril Castle** perched on the cliffs, right.

3 As you gain height the gorge shallows. Go through a bridle gate in the dry-stone wall on the right, and follow the well-defined track across high pastureland. It passes through a gate in another wall before being joined by a path that has descended the grassy hillside on the right. The track divides soon after the junction. Take the left fork, uphill, slightly away from the wall on the right to the top corner of the field. Go through the gate here and follow a short stretch of walled track to a crossroads of routes near the old **Hazard Mine**.

4 Turn right through the gate here along a stony walled lane, which swings right

to reach the B6061 near **Oxlow House Farm**. Take the path beyond the right-hand gate across the road to pass the disused quarry on **Windy Knoll**.

5 Just before the road turn right on a grassy path parallel to the road. Join the road at a gate and turn left, then fork right down the lane for **Blue John Cavern**.

6 After 400yds (366m) turn right down the tarmac road to the **Blue John Cavern**, then left by the ticket office. Cross the stile in the fence and trace the path as it crosses several fields. Beyond a stile the path arcs right, traversing precipitous grassy hillslopes. Pass the **Treak Cliff Cavern** ticket office. Go left down concrete steps by the ticket office, then right on a concrete path with handrails.

7 Go through a gap in this handrail and follow a narrow cross-field path by a collapsed wall. On the approach to **Speedwell Cavern** the path becomes indistinct. Take an obvious gate straight ahead on to the **Winnats Pass Road**.

8 A path on the far side takes the route through **Longcliff Estate**. It roughly follows the line of a wall and veers left beneath the hillslopes of **Cow Low** to reach **Goosehill Hall**. Here, follow Goosehill (a lane), back into **Castleton**. Beyond **Goosehill Bridge**, turn left down a surfaced streamside path to the car park.

what to look for

Treak Cliff Cavern is one of the best places to see fossils. In the limestone you can study the remains of sea creatures that accumulated in the bed of a tropical sea 320 million years ago.

Castle Hotel

Unpretentious, yet full of character, this rambling, part 17th-century inn can be found tucked away from the main village road opposite the superb medieval church. Beyond the stone-built façade there's an inviting, stone-flagged bar with stone walls, carved beams, old pews and a magnificent open log fire. Equally comfortable adjoining rooms have open fires, a good mix of tables and chairs and walls lined with prints and old photographs of Castleton. Deep bay windows overlook the street and church, while outside there's a super heated terrace and a pretty garden with rural views.

Food

Good value bar food ranges from sausages and mustard mash with rich onion gravy, and chicken pie and Cajun salmon salad on the printed menu, to rump steak salad and chicken, bacon and avocado salad on the specials board. There is a separate sandwich menu.

about the pub

Castle Hotel
Castle Street, Castleton
Hope Valley, Derbyshire S33 8WG
Tel 01433 620578

DIRECTIONS: in the village centre, set back off the main road and opposite the church – see Getting to the start

PARKING: 20, or use main village car park

OPEN: daily, all day

FOOD: all day

BREWERY/COMPANY: Mitchells & Butler

REAL ALE: Bass, Tetley, John Smiths, guest beer

DOGS: on leads in garden only

ROOMS: 12 en suite

Family facilities

Children are welcome inside away from the bar and they have a good children's menu to choose from. There is a garden and terrace for fine days.

Alternative refreshment stops

There are plenty of tea shops, cafés, restaurants and pubs in Castleton

☛ Where to go from here

Besides the caverns seen on the route (Treak Cliff Cavern is one of the best places to see fossils), make time to visit Peveril Castle in the village. It has a Norman keep and enjoys spectacular views over the village and up Cavedale(www.english-heritage.org.uk).

Miller's Dale

The rural serenity of modern Miller's Dale belies its early role in the Industrial Revolution.

Miller's Dale

It's all quiet in Miller's Dale these days, but it wasn't always so. Many early industrialists wanted to build their cotton mills in the countryside, far away from the marauding Luddites of the city. The Wye and its tributaries had the power to work these mills. The railway followed, and that brought more industry with it. And so little Miller's Dale and its neighbours joined the Industrial Revolution. The walk starts in Tideswell Dale. Nowadays it's choked with thickets and herbs but they hide a history of quarrying and mining. Here the miners wanted basalt, a dark, hard igneous rock that was used for road building.

Today's smart apartments belie the gruesome past at Litton Mill. The Memoirs of Robert Blincoe, written in 1863, tells of mill owner Ellis Needham's cruelty to child apprentices, who were often shipped in from the poorhouses of London. Many of the children died and were buried in the churchyards of Tideswell and Taddington. It is said that ghosts of some of the apprentices still make appearances in or around the mill. The walk emerges from the shadows of the mill into Water-cum-Jolly Dale. At first the river is lined by mudbanks thick with rushes and common horsetail. It's popular with wildfowl. The river widens out and, at the same time, impressive limestone cliffs squeeze the path. The river's widening is artificial, a result of it being controlled to form a head of water for the downstream mill.

Round the next corner is Cressbrook Mill, built by Sir Richard Arkwright, but taken over by William Newton. Newton also employed child labour but was said to have treated them well. The rooftop bell tower would have peeled to beckon the apprentices, who lived next door, to the works. Like Litton, this impressive Georgian mill was allowed to moulder, but is now restored as flats. The walk leaves the banks of the Wye at Cressbrook to take in pretty Cressbrook Dale. In this nature reserve you'll see lily-of-the-valley, wild garlic, bee and fragrant orchids. Just as you think you've found your true rural retreat you'll climb to the rim of the dale. Look across it and see the grassed-over spoil heaps of lead mines. Finally, the ancient strip fields of Litton form a mosaic of pasture and dry-stone walls on the return to Tideswell Dale.

the walk

1 Follow the path southwards from beside the car park's toilet block into **Tideswell Dale**, taking the right-hand fork to cross over the little bridge.

2 On entering **Miller's Dale**, go left on the tarmac lane to **Litton Mill**. Go through the gateposts on to a concessionary path through the mill yard. Beyond the mill, the path follows the **River Wye** as it meanders through the tight, steep-sided dale.

3 The river widens out in **Water-cum-Jolly Dale** and the path, liable to flooding here, traces a wall of limestone cliffs before reaching Cressbrook. Do not cross the bridge on the right, but turn left to pass behind **Cressbrook Mill** to the road.

3h00	6 MILES	9.7 KM	LEVEL 2

4 Turn left along the road, then take the right fork which climbs steadily into **Cressbrook Dale**. Where the road doubles back uphill leave it for a track going straight ahead into the woods. At a major fork keep right; the track degenerates into a narrow path that emerges in a clearing high above the stream. Follow it downhill to a footbridge over the stream, then take the right fork path, which climbs high up the valley side to a stile in the top wall. (To omit a very steep climb to a viewpoint here, follow the valley-bottom path at the fork past the footbridge to rejoin the route at the stepping stones in Point 5).

5 Do not cross the stile, but take the downhill path to the dale bottom, where there's a junction of paths. The one wanted here re-crosses the stream on stepping stones, and climbs into **Tansley Dale**.

6 The path turns right at the top of the dale, follows a tumbledown wall before crossing it on a step stile. Head for a wall corner in the next field, then veer right through a narrow enclosure to reach a walled track just south of **Litton village**.

7 Turn left along the track, which comes out on to a country lane at the crown of a sharp bend. Keep straight on along the lane but leave it at the next bend for a cross-field path to **Bottomhill Road**. Across the road, a field path descends to the lane at **Dale House Farm**. Turn left, then right on a lane marked unsuitable for motors. Follow this road into **Tideswell**.

8 After looking around the village head south down the main street, then right

MAP: OS Explorer OL24 White Peak

START/FINISH: Tideswell Dale pay car park, grid ref SK 154743

PATHS: generally well-defined paths and tracks, path in Water-cum-Jolly Dale liable to flooding, 12 stiles and gates

LANDSCAPE: limestone dales

PUBLIC TOILETS: at car park

TOURIST INFORMATION: Buxton, tel 01298 25106

THE PUB: George Hotel, Commercial Road, see Point **8** on route

🛈 There is a particularly steep section of the route at Point **4** which we recommend that families with young children avoid by remaining on the valley floor path. If the River Wye is running high and brown then the route will be impassable at Water-cum-Jolly Dale, Point **3**

Getting to the start

Tideswell is just south of the A623 between Chapel-en-le-Frith and Baslow. Look for the 'Cathedral of the Peak' brown tourist signs. Pass through Tideswell and continue downhill, bending right into Tideswell Dale. The car park (well signed) is nearly a mile (1.6km) south.

Researched and written by:
Neil Coates, John Gillham

20

👫👫
WALK

Miller's Dale

DERBYSHIRE

on to **Gordon Road** (in front of the **Horse and Jockey pub**), which then heads south.

9 Where this ends, continue down the stony track ahead, which runs parallel with the main road. At a gate keep left to find a waymarked handgate; the path then drops gradually to a stile on to the road just above the treatment works. Turn right along the road; in 150yds (137m) take a path off a rough pull-in, left, to join a path back to the car park.

what to look for

Cressbrook Dale is part of the Derbyshire Dales National Nature Reserve. On the limestone grassland you may see orchids, cranesbill, mountain pansy, globeflower and spring sandwort. One of the many limestone-loving plants is the Nottingham catchfly, which loves dry, stony places. The white flowers roll back in daytime, but are fragrant at night. Small insects are often caught on the sticky stalks but nature is being wasteful, for they're never devoured by the plant.

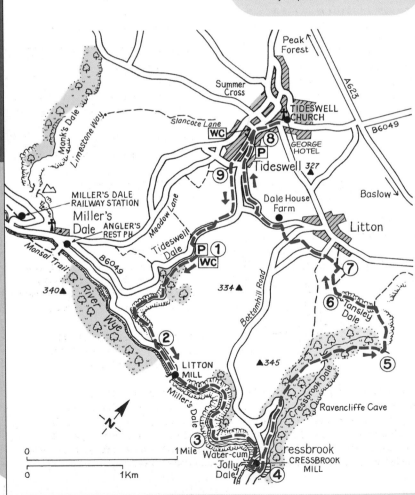

George Hotel

Locate Tideswell's famous parish church and you will find this unpretentious stone-built pub-hotel, its creeper-clad façade festooned with colourful hanging baskets and window boxes in season. A warm welcome awaits walkers in the traditional L-shaped bar lounge/dining area, with its comfortable upholstered wall benches, simple pub tables and chairs, and walls lined with old village photographs and quality local watercolours (for sale). The separate, quarry-tiled taproom is popular with local drinkers. The sheltered rear garden has been created from the old stabling yard; tables to the front overlook the village.

about the pub

George Hotel
Commercial Road, Tideswell
Buxton, Derbyshire SK17 8NU
Tel 01298 871382
www.george-hotel-tideswell.co.uk

DIRECTIONS: centre of Tideswell next to the church. See Getting to the start

PARKING: 20

OPEN: daily, all day Saturday and Sunday

FOOD: daily, all day Saturday and Sunday in summer

BREWERY/COMPANY: Hardy & Hanson

REAL ALE: Hardy & Hanson Best, Old Trip, seasonal ale

DOGS: welcome in the pub

ROOMS: 5 bedrooms

Food

Reliable, traditional pub meals come in the form of steak and ale pie, seafood crumble, lasagne and a good range of sandwiches and filled jacket potatoes. Blackboard specials may include beef bourguignon and monkfish in Pernod on a bed of fennel.

Family facilities

Children are made most welcome, as long as they keep away from the bar, and they have a standard children's menu to choose from. There is good outdoor seating.

Alternative refreshment stops

Angler's Rest at Miller's Dale, Hills and Dales Tea rooms in Tideswell.

☛ Where to go from here

Miller's Dale Railway Station (the line closed in 1967), just off the route, is a fascinating old site with a good deal of information on the railway, the wildlife and walks in the area.

Long Dale

DERBYSHIRE

Long Dale and the White Peak

From the Tissington Trail on to peaceful backroads near Hartington, returning via Long Dale and the new Pennine Bridleway.

Fossils

The main reason for building the railway on what is now the High Peak Trail was to move limestone from quarries to canals and lowland railways. The line itself burrows through cuttings and across embankments of limestone, and embedded in the limestone you'll find fossils of the creatures that lived in the shallow tropical seas that covered this area 300 million years ago. The most recognisable are the remains of crinoids. These were a kind of primitive starfish that attached themselves to rocks by a cord made up of small segments. It is these that you'll find in blocks and slabs of limestone, often in great numbers and looking like the mixed up contents of a necklace box. Belemnites are another fossil that are also found in numbers here. The fossil is that of the shell and looks very like a bullet casing!

On warm and sunny summer days stop for a break in Long Dale and take a close look at the limestone walls, where you may be lucky enough to catch a glimpse of a common lizard basking in the heat. Only about 4in (10cm) long, they're very agile and the slightest movement will see them disappear into the wall crevices and cracks they call home.

the ride

1 From **Parsley Hay** head south along the **High Peak Trail**. The firm, level surface means you can concentrate on the views as much as the way ahead – but look out for walkers and horse riders, as this is a multi-user trail.

2 In a short distance the route forks; keep right here, joining the **Tissington Trail**, the former trackbed of the line down to Ashbourne. Passing through a deep cutting, the trail emerges to reveal good views across towards the Staffordshire Moors. Shortly, to your left, the distinct hill is **Lean Low**, the burial site of our distant forefathers – a tumulus, or burial mound, was found on this windswept summit. The trail sweeps close to **Hartington-moor Farm** before crossing a bridge and reaching the former **Hartington Station**.

3 Take time to explore the site here before continuing south – and start counting the bridges. At the **seventh bridge** – three over you, four that you cross – you need to dismount and wheel your bike down the footpath on the right. There's a **barn** and trees off to the right and an old **quarry** to the left as additional locator points (if you reach the main road on your left you've gone too far). This drops to a quiet lane bound for **Biggin-by-Hartington** and is now your route to the left, a long and very gentle climb between the characteristic walled pastures and hay meadows of this fertile plateau. Cresting a low ridge, splendid views open out across the western Peak District and ahead to **Biggin**.

4 To visit **Biggin** itself you can divert right along **Drury Lane** to find the village shop and the **Waterloo Inn** (to return to the main route just pass by the pub on your right, the main route then comes in from the left at a junction). The main route avoids the village and descends to a couple of sharp bends at **Cotterill Farm** before reaching a junction. Keep ahead here (the village option rejoins here) to and straight through the next junction (pond on the right). An easy, all-but-level stretch ends with a narrow descent down **Harding's Lane** to a junction with the B5054.

5 Take great care crossing here; it's easiest to cycle down the main road a few yards to allow a clear view of traffic before crossing into the lane directly opposite. This is the start of a delightful, easy ascent along the valley floor of **Long Dale**. The lane meanders lazily beneath limestone crags and screes, imperceptibly rising for about 2 miles (3.2km) where a lane joins from the left. Ignore this and keep ahead, passing **Vincent House Farm** to a junction. You can turn right here to return to Parsley Hay, but continuing along the main lane allows you to visit a fine country pub.

6 The lane continues to rise gently, soon leaving the dale behind, unveiling views across the Staffordshire moorlands. Ignore the next turn right and continue to a crossroads at **High Needham**. Here turn right along an undulating road to reach the **Royal Oak** pub at **Hurdlow**, which is adjacent to the **High Peak Trail**. Pick up the Trail beyond the old **railway bridge** and head south to return the last 2 miles (3.2km) to **Parsley Hay**.

3h30 — 12 MILES — 19.3 KM — LEVEL 2

MAP: OS Explorer OL24 White Peak
START/FINISH: Parsley Hay on the High Peak Trail, grid ref SK147637
TRAILS/TRACKS: partly along the High Peak, then Tissington trails and along usually quiet minor roads.
LANDSCAPE: the route winds across the limestone plateau of the White Peak and includes an easy ride up a superb, shallow limestone dry-valley.
PUBLIC TOILETS: at Parsley Hay
TOURIST INFORMATION: Bakewell, tel 01629 813227
CYCLE HIRE: Derbyshire County Council centre at Parsley Hay, tel 01298 84493 www.derbyshire.gov.uk/countryside
THE PUB: The Royal Oak, Hurdlow, see point 6 on route

One crossing of the B5054 near Hartington requires particular care. Walkers and horse-riders also use the High Peak Trail. Suitable for family groups who have some experience with on-road cycling, best tackled by older children

Getting to the start
Parsley Hay Centre is on the High Peak Trail and is signposted off the A515 Buxton to Ashbourne road. There is a pay car park here.

Why do this cycle ride?
A good mix of railway trackbed and some quiet by-roads that thread between stone villages, make this an easy ride on the White Peak's limestone plateau. With glimpses into some of the deeper dales, your main preoccupation may be in identifying some of the knolls and hills that form a wide horizon, while Long Dale is an enchanting stretch up a valley with wild flowers in the summer.

Researched and written by: Neil Coates

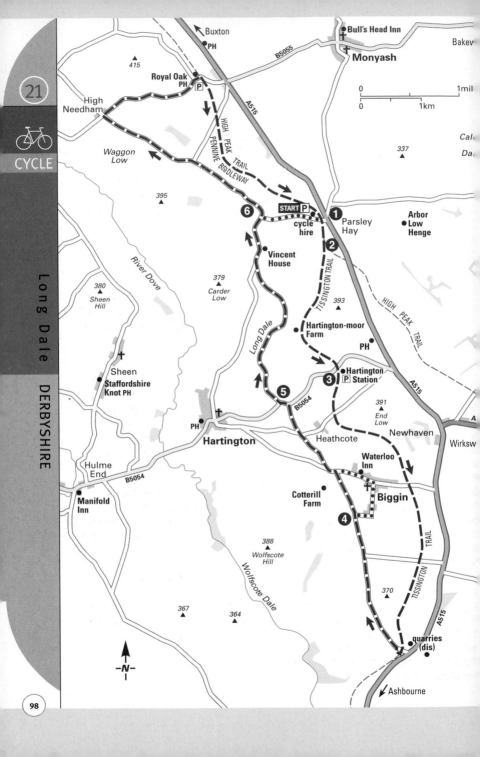

Long Dale   DERBYSHIRE

↑ Buxton

Bull's Head Inn
PH
✝ **Monyash**   Bakew

B5055

415 ▲

Royal Oak
PH P

High
Needham

A515

HIGH PEAK TRAIL
PENNINE BRIDLEWAY

*Waggon
Low*

337 ▲   Cale
                         Da

395 ▲

6

START P

cycle
hire

1 Parsley
    Hay

2

Arbor
● **Low**
  Henge

● **Vincent
  House**

River Dove

379 ▲
*Carder
Low*

TISSINGTON TRAIL

393 ▲

HIGH PEAK TRAIL

380 ▲
*Sheen
Hill*

Long Dale

● **Hartington-moor
  Farm**

PH ●

A515

✝
● **Sheen**
**Staffordshire
Knot PH**

5

B5054

3 ● **Hartington**
    P **Station**

391 ▲
*End
Low*

Newhaven

Wirksw

PH ●

✝

Hartington

Heathcote

**Waterloo
Inn**

A

**Hulme
End**

B5054

● **Manifold
  Inn**

● **Cotterill
  Farm**

✝
Biggin

4

388 ▲
*Wolfscote
Hill*

Wolfscote Dale

370 ▲

TISSINGTON TRAIL

A515

367 ▲

364 ▲

↑
–N–
|

**quarries
(dis)** ●

↓ Ashbourne

0 ─── 1mil
0 ─── 1km

Royal Oak

about the pub

Royal Oak
Hurdlow, Buxton
Derbyshire SK17 9QJ
Tel 01298 83288

DIRECTIONS: from Parsley Hay car park turn left to the A515. Turn left towards Buxton. In about 1.75 miles (2.8km) turn left towards Longnor. The Royal Oak is just across the railway bridge next to the Hurdlow car park on the High Peak Trail

PARKING: 30

OPEN: daily, all day

FOOD: daily, all day

BREWERY/COMPANY: free house

REAL ALE: Bass, Marston's Pedigree, guest beer

Just as it did when it was built some 200 years ago, the Royal Oak continues to serve railway users, although today it provides welcome refreshment to weary walkers and cyclists tackling the High Peak Trail, a 17-mile (27km) route that follows the old trackbed. (There are cycle lock up and securing posts in the car park.) From the outside it may look a little time-worn but inside it's a fine place, with simply furnished rooms on several levels, two bars and a dining area, all with great views of the surrounding countryside. A blazing log fire in a grand stone fireplace warms the lounge bar in winter. Brass jugs, copper kettles and horsebrasses hang from the beams, while in the lounge the walls are decorated with old golf clubs and country paintings. There is a cellar pool room.

Food
From a standard menu you can order fresh cod and chips, loin of pork with apple sauce, beef and Stilton pie, salmon and broccoli pasta, curries, hot rolls and filled jacket potatoes. Blackboard daily specials favour fresh fish dishes.

Family facilities
Older children can make good use of the pool table in the cellar. Children of all ages are very welcome throughout the pub and younger ones have their own standard menu to choose from. Good summer alfresco seating on two grassy areas, both with country views.

Alternative refreshment stops
There are pubs at Biggin (Waterloo Inn), Sparklow (Royal Oak); snacks at Parsley Hay; several pubs and cafés in Hartington, just off the route.

☞ Where to go from here
Arbor Low Henge, a major Neolithic site near to Parsley Hay, is a significant stone circle although the stones are now lying flat. Small charge for entry.

Wolfscote Dale and a Railway Trail

WALK

Wolfscote Dale and Biggin Dale wind through the heart of the upland limestone country.

Compleat Angler

From its source, on Axe Edge, to Hartington the River Dove is little more than a stream, flowing past the dragon's back at Chrome Hill, and in an attractive but shallow valley south of Crowdecote. Once through the pretty woodlands of Beresford Dale it cuts a deep limestone canyon with with cliffs and tors almost equal to those of Dovedale. This canyon is Wolfscote Dale, and it is wilder and more unspoiled than Dovedale with narrower, less populated paths, and less woodland to hide the crags. Weirs have been constructed to create calm pools that attract trout and grayling to linger.

The river was a joy to Charles Cotton, a 17th-century poet born in nearby Beresford Hall. Cotton, an enthusiastic angler, introduced Izaak Walton to the area and taught him the art of fly-fishing. Together they built a fishing temple in the woods of Beresford Dale (in private grounds.) They wrote *The Compleat Angler*, a collection of fishing stories published in 1651.

The path up Wolfscote Dale begins at Lode Mill, which still has its waterwheel intact. The river, verged by lush vegetation, has cut a deep and twisting valley through the limestone. The slopes are wooded with ash, sycamore and alder. Further north this woodland thins out to reveal more of the crags, and a ravine opens out to the right of Coldeaton Bridge. The dale, like so many in Derbyshire, is rich in wildlife. Dipper, pied wagtails and grey wagtails often forage along the limestone banks, and if you're quick enough you may see a kingfisher diving for a fish. The dale divides again beneath the magnificent Peaseland Rocks. It's a shame to leave the Dove but Biggin Dale is a pleasing contrast. For most of the year it's a dry valley, but in winter the rocky path may be jostling for room with a newly surfaced stream. It's a narrow dale with limestone screes and scrub gorse.

Through a gate you enter a National Nature Reserve, known for its many species of limestone-loving plants and its butterflies At the top of the dale you come to Biggin, a straggling village, from where the return route is an easy-paced one, using the Tissington Trail, which ambles over the high plains of Alsop Moor.

the walk

1 From the car park at **Alsop Old Station**, cross the busy A515 road and follow the **Milldale Road** immediately opposite. Bear right at the junction; in about 200yds (183m) the option of a parallel footpath, left, keeps you safe from the traffic.

2 On reaching the bottom of the dale by **Lode Mill**, turn right along the footpath,

what to look for

In Biggin Dale, there are rampantly prickly gorse bushes as well as many limestone-loving plants including the purple-flowered meadow cranesbill, patches of delicate harebells, early purple orchids with their dark-spotted stems and leaves and the distinctive orangy-yellow cowslips.

tracing the river's east bank through a winding, partially wooded valley.

3 Ignore the footpath on the right at **Coldeaton Bridge**, but instead stay with **Wolfscote Dale** beneath thickly wooded slopes on the right. Beyond a stile the woods cease and the dale becomes bare and rock-fringed, with a cave on the right and the bold pinnacles of **Peaseland Rocks** ahead. Here the valley sides open out into the dry valley of **Biggin Dale**, where this route goes next.

4 The unsignposted path into **Biggin Dale** begins beyond a stile in a cross-wall and climbs by that wall. It continues through scrub woodland and beneath limestone screes. Beyond a gate you enter a nature reserve.

5 There's another gate at the far end of the nature reserve. Beyond it the dale curves left, then right, before dividing again beneath the hill pastures of **Biggin Grange**. We divert left here, over a stile to follow the footpath, signposted to **Hartington**. On the other side of the wall there's a concrete dewpond.

6 After 200yds (183m) there's another junction of paths. This time ignore the one signposted to **Hartington** and keep walking straight on up the shallowing dale, following the path to **Biggin**. It stays with the valley round to the right, passing a small sewage works (on the left) before

Left and below: Wolfscote Dale

4h00 · **7.5 MILES** · **12.1 KM** · **LEVEL 1** 2 3

MAP: OS Explorer OL24 White Peak

START/FINISH: Tissington Trail pay car park at Alsop Old Station, grid ref SK 156549

PATHS: generally well-defined paths, about 20 stiles and gates

LANDSCAPE: partially wooded limestone dales and high pasture

PUBLIC TOILETS: none on route

TOURIST INFORMATION: Ashbourne, tel 01335 343666

THE PUB: The Waterloo Inn, Biggin-by-Hartington, see Point **7** on route

 Limestone dale sides can be slippery after rain

Getting to the Start

The walk begins at Alsop Old Station, one of the former station sites on the Tissington Trail. It is signposted off the A515 about 6 miles (9.7km) north of Ashbourne.

Researched and written by:
Neil Coates, John Gillham

climbing out of the dale to reach the road at **Dale End**.

7 Turn right along the road for a few paces then left, following a road past the **Waterloo Inn** and through **Biggin** village.

8 Turn right again 500yds (457m) from the village centre on a path that climbs to the **Tissington Trail**. Follow this trackbed southwards across the pastures of **Biggin** and **Alsop** moors. After 2 miles (3.2km) you reach the car park at **Alsop Old Station**.

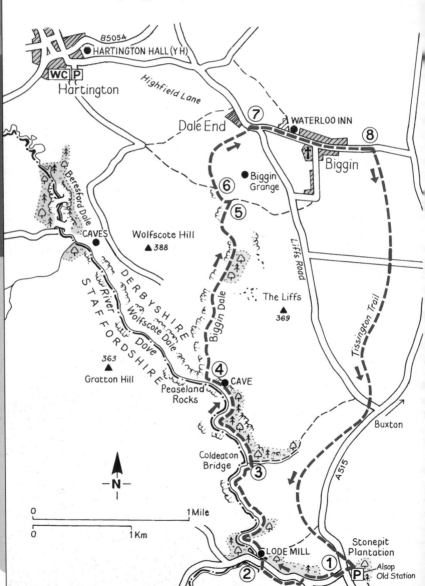

Waterloo Inn

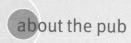

Don't be put off by the grey pebble-dashed exterior of the Waterloo Inn – inside you'll find the atmosphere of a friendly and welcoming village pub. Well loved by locals and passing walkers alike, it comprises a quarry-tiled bar, wall-bench seating and traditional pub tables and chairs. There is a separate carpeted lounge area and a very popular pool room. It is a handy refuelling spot midway through this walk – a place to stop and savour a pint of Black Sheep Bitter in the garden on fine sunny days.

Food

As befits a homely village the local food is no-nonsense, good-value pub fare. Here you'll find an all-day breakfast, fish and chips, lasagne, a range of sandwiches and pizzas, and the occasional daily special such as lamb shank with mint gravy.

Family facilities

Children are welcome throughout the pub and have their own standard menu.

Alternative refreshment stops

The Blue Bell at Tissington Gate is a couple of miles south along the A515.

☞ Where to go from here

Experience the atmosphere of a working 18th-century cotton mill at Masson Mills Working Textile Museum in Matlock Bath (www.massonmills.co.uk).

about the pub

WATERLOO INN
Biggin-by-Hartington, Buxton
Derbyshire SK17 0DH
Tel 01298 84284

DIRECTIONS: On Point **7** on the route. By car, Biggin is signposted left off the A515, north of Ashbourne

PARKING: 20

OPEN: daily, all day Friday, Saturday and Sunday

FOOD: daily

BREWERY/COMPANY: Enterprise Inns

REAL ALE: Black Sheep Bitter and Special, guest beers

DOGS: welcome throughout

Wolfscote Dale

Dovedale

A walk through the alpine-like splendour of the Peak District's most famous dale.

Ivory Spires and Wooded Splendour

Right from the start there's drama as you follow the River Dove, wriggling through a narrow gorge between Bunster Hill and the towering pyramid of Thorpe Cloud. A limestone path urges you to climb to a bold rocky outcrop high above the river. Lovers' Leap has a fine view across the dale to pinnacles of the Twelve Apostles. It's a view to gladden your hearts – not the sort of

place you'd think of throwing yourself from at all. However, in 1761 an Irish dean and his lady companion, who were out horse riding fell off the rock. The dean died of his injuries but the lady survived to tell the tale.

The Dove writhes round another corner. Above your heads, flaky fingers of limestone known as the Tissington Spires rise out from thick woodland cover. Just a few footsteps away on the right there's a splendid natural arch, which is just outside the entrance to Reynard's Cave. This is the result of the cave's roof collapsing. The dale's limestone walls close in and the

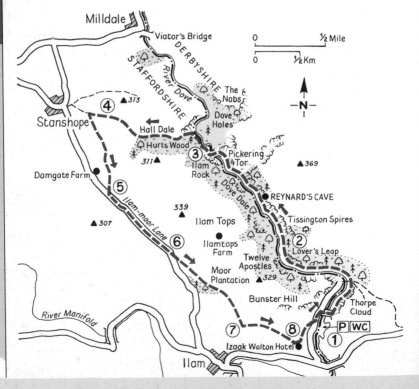

path climbs to a place more remote from the rushing river, which often floods around here. As the valley opens out again two gigantic rock stacks face each other across the Dove. Pickering Tor has a small cave at its foot. A little footbridge allows you across to the other side to the foot of Ilam Rock. This 8oft (25m) leaning thumb of limestone has an overhang on the south side that's popular with climbers. It too has a cave at the bottom, which is only 4ft (1.2m) at the entrance but opens out to over 3oft (10m) inside. You will get a better view of them when you cross the little footbridge to the cave at the foot of the rocks. On this side you're in Staffordshire and the paths are less populated.

The continuing walk into Hall Dale heralds a less formal landscape. The dale is dry and it climbs up the hillside. Here is Hurts Wood which has wych elm, whitebeam, ash and rowan. Some fences have kept grazing animals out, allowing the trees and shrubs to regenerate.

Top: Looking across Dovedale
Below: Crossing the stepping stones at Dovedale

3h30 — **5 MILES** — **8 KM** — **LEVEL 123**

MAP: OS Explorer OL24 White Peak
START/FINISH: Dovedale car park, near Thorpe, grid ref SK 146509
PATHS: mostly good paths, lanes, 20 stiles and handgates
LANDSCAPE: partially wooded dales, and high pastures
PUBLIC TOILETS: at car park
TOURIST INFORMATION: Ashbourne, tel 01335 343666
THE PUB: The Izaak Walton Hotel, Dovedale, see Point **8** on route
❶ One steep scramble up on to ridge top below Bunster Hill (Point **7**)

Getting to the start
Dovedale is signed off the A515 road 2 miles (3.2km) north of Ashbourne. Follow the signs along narrow minor roads (beware of coaches) to the signed National Trust Car Park on a No Through Road at the foot of Dovedale. The Izaak Walton Hotel is also off this road.

Researched and written by:
Neil Coates, John Gillham

You'll hear and see many birds – warblers, redstarts and black caps; and you'll see wild flowers – dog's mercury, wood anemone and wood forget-me-not.

It seems a shame to leave the dale behind but soon you're walking down a quiet lane with Ilam and the beautiful Manifold Valley on your right and a shapely peak, Bunster Hill, on your left. A path takes you across the shoulder of the hill, across the ridge and furrow of a medieval field system, then back into the valley of the Dove.

the walk

1 Turn right out of the car park and follow the road along the west bank of the **Dove**. Cross the footbridge to the opposite bank and turn left along a wide footpath. This twists and turns through the narrow dale, between **Bunster Hill** and **Thorpe Cloud**.

2 Follow the path as it climbs some steps up through the woods on to the justifiably famous rocky outcrop of **Lovers' Leap**, then descends past the magnificent **Tissington Spires** and **Reynard's Cave**. Here a huge natural arch surrounds the much smaller entrance to the historic cave. As the dale narrows the path climbs above the river.

3 The dale widens again. Leave the main path for a route signposted '**To Stanshope**', and cross the footbridge over the Dove. A narrow woodland path turns right beneath the huge spire of **Ilam Rock** above you. Beyond a squeeze stile the path eases to the left into **Hall Dale**. Following the valley bottom and a stone wall on the left, it climbs out of the woods into a rugged limestone-cragged gorge.

4 The gorge shallows before leaving the National Trust estate at a stile. Continue ahead until **Stanshope** hamlet is

what to look for

The Dove is a clear, pure river with lots of wildlife both in and around the water. Brown trout and grayling feed on the caddis flies and mayflies, while if you're lucky, you may see a kingfisher diving for a minnow or a bullhead.

well in view. At a crossing of paths marked by a tall waymark post turn left through a stile and go ahead, with a wall off to your left, to another stile. Keep in line towards the lone barn on the horizon, with a wall on your right. Where this turns away, keep ahead to a stile. Turn right to a handgate beneath trees. Head half left to a handgate in the far corner, then a further one in 50yds (46m). From here head half left again to a stile into a metalled lane.

5 Turn left along the quiet country lane. There are magnificent views from here down to Ilam and the Manifold Valley ahead of you and down to the right.

6 After 800yds (732m) take a footpath on the left, just before the driveway for Air Cottage Farm. Cut across the driveway and climb the stile just right of an open gateway. A field path now heads roughly south east, traversing low grassy fellsides to the top of **Moor Plantation** woods and a corner stone step stile.

7 The path (a scramble where it has fallen away in places – take care) cuts across the steep sides of **Bunster Hill**, before straddling its south spur and descending to a step-stile in the intake wall. A clear path now descends south east across sloping pastures to the back of the **Izaak Walton Hotel**.

8 From here head towards the jaws of Dovedale across two more fields and back to the car park.

Izaak Walton Hotel

Named after the renowned author of The Compleat Angler, *it is said that Izaak himself used to break his journey here to fish the River Blythe. Believed to date back to the mid-17th century, recent refurbishment has recaptured its roots and it now is more an upmarket hotel than a pub. However, at the heart of the place (and welcoming walkers) is the Dovedale Bar, a comfortable public bar with a crackling log fire in a massive stone fireplace, heavy beamed ceilings, fishing prints and framed trout flies on the walls. The cosy adjoining room is filled with old pews and carved settles. On fine days take your pint of Tiger out to the spacious lawned gardens and savour the jaw-dropping views of Dovedale.*

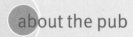

about the pub

Izaak Walton Hotel
Dovedale, Ashbourne
Derbyshire DE6 2AY
Tel 01335 350555
www.izaakwaltonhotel.com

DIRECTIONS: see Getting to the start of the walk	
PARKING: 60	
OPEN: daily	
FOOD: daily	
BREWERY/COMPANY: free house	
REAL ALE: Everard's Tiger, guest beer	
DOGS: welcome throughout the hotel	
ROOMS: 34 en suite	

Food

In addition to a good range of sandwiches and home-made soups (carrot and ginger), you'll find the Izaak Walton burger, served with bacon, Stilton and red onion marmalade; pasta with roasted vegetables and pesto, and oak smoked salmon on the main menu. Daily dishes may include lamb cutlets with onion gravy and garlic mash, and sea bass with prawn and lobster sauce.

Family facilities

There are lawned gardens to explore on fine days. The standard children's menu includes fish fingers and burgers with chips.

Alternative refreshment stops

The Bluebell Inn at nearby Tissington offers bar and restaurant meals.

☞ Where to go from here

To the south west is Alton Towers with its exhilarating rides and attractions (www.altontowers.com). Sudbury Hall and the Museum of Childhood is to the south (www.nationaltrust.org.uk).

Over Win Hill

WALK

Following ancient roads to the site of an ancient battle, via the Roman fort at Navio.

Marching Roads and Battlefields

This walk from Hope to Win Hill threads through pastures above the River Noe. Here you're treading the same ground as Roman soldiers and Celtic and Saxon warriors before you. Down in the valley below a furious tribal battle ended in victory for King Athelstan, grandson of Alfred the Great. He would soon become the first Saxon ruler of all England.

In one of those riverside fields the path comes across the earthwork remains of the Roman fort, Navio. Built in the time of Emperor Antoninus Pius, the fort stood at a junction of roads serving garrisons at Buxton, Glossop, and Templeborough. At its peak it would have sheltered over 500 soldiers. It remained occupied until the 4th century, controlling the rich mining area around the Peak. Many Roman relics found near the fort can be viewed at the Buxton Museum. Win Hill looms large in your thoughts as you cross to the other side of the valley and climb towards it. As you're passing through the hamlet of Aston take a quick look at Aston Hall. Built in 1578, it has an unusual pedimented window with a weather-worn carved figure. The doorway is surrounded by Roman Doric columns and a four-centred arch.

Beyond the hall the climb begins in earnest up a stony track, then through bracken and grass hillside where Win Hill's rocky summit peeps out across the heathered ridge. A concrete trig point caps the rocks. And what a view to reward your efforts! The Ladybower Reservoir's sinuous shorelines creep between dark spruce woods, while the gritstone tors of Kinder Scout, the Derwent Edge, and Bleaklow fill the northern horizon, framed by the pyramidal Lose Hill.

There are several theories on how Win Hill got its name. The most likely one is that it derives from an earlier name, Wythinehull, which meant Willow Hill. The one I prefer though concerns two warlords, Edwin, the first Christian king of Northumbria, and Cuicholm, King of Wessex. Cuicholm murdered Lilla, Edwin's maidservant, and Edwin was looking for revenge. Cuicholm assembled his forces on Lose Hill, while his enemy camped on Win Hill. Edwin, was victorious and thus his hill was named Win Hill.

Now you follow Edwin down the hill, before continuing across the Hope Valley fields back to Hope.

Top right: Hope Valley
Right: St Peter's church in Hope village

what to look for

Hope is on the edge of limestone country. Often you can see the change in the dry-stone walls. Those in the valley are made from paler limestone, while those on the Win Hill slopes are of the darker gritstone. These walls were mostly built between 1780 and 1820, when enclosure of upland areas was taking place at a prolific rate right across the country. Although expensive to build and repair, they are now considered to be an integral part of the Peakland landscape and various conservation bodies devote time to training new generations of skilled wallers.

the walk

3h00 **4.75 MILES** **7.7 KM** **LEVEL 2**

1 Turn right out of the car park along Hope's main street. At the crossroads beside the **church**, turn right along **Pindale Road**. Cross the river bridge and continue along the lane to the next left turn, **Eccles Lane**. Turn along this.

2 After about 100yds (91m), go over a stile by a gate and follow the path running roughly parallel to the lane at first, then the **River Noe**, to reach the site of the Roman fort of **Navio**. Beyond the earthworks go over a stile in a fence and bear half right across another field to reach the B6049 road at **Brough**.

3 Turn left through the village and cross the footbridge over the **River Noe** just past the agricultural merchant's mill. Go left over a stile and head north west to the A625. Turn left along the road for 200yds (183m) to a small gate just beyond a cottage. Follow the fence and brook on the right to pass to the right of some houses.

4 Turn left along the lane towards the **railway station**, then go right along a narrow path which leads to a footbridge over the line. Cross the **bridge** and turn right at its far end, then left through a handgate to cross yet more fields, this time keeping the fence on your right and ignoring a stile footbridge on the right.

5 When you reach **Aston** turn left along the road, then almost immediately turn right along a narrow, surfaced lane, signposted **'Win Hill & Hope Cross'**.

MAP: OS Explorer OL1 Dark Peak; grid ref SK 172835

START/FINISH: Hope pay car park

PATHS: paths can be slippery after rain, around 23 gates and stiles

LANDSCAPE: riverside pastureland and high peak

PUBLIC TOILETS: at car park

TOURIST INFORMATION: Castleton, tel 01433 620679

THE PUB: Cheshire Cheese Inn, Edale Road, Hope, just off Point **8** on route

🛈 The short scramble up to the summit of Win Hill is steep. Take care crossing the main road near Brough

Getting to the start

From Sheffield take the A625 south west and turn on to the A6187 near Hathersage, following the brown tourist signs for the Caverns at Castleton. The main car park in Hope is through the village and on the right.

Researched and written by:
Neil Coates, John Gillham

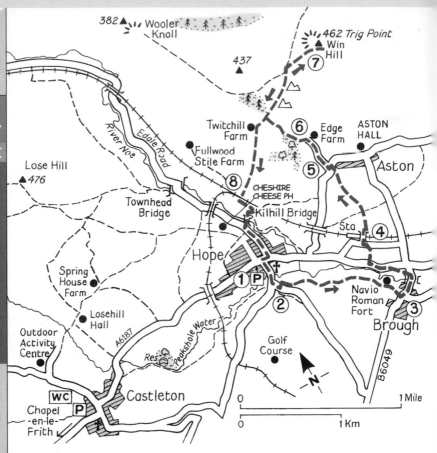

6 In front of **Edge Farm** an unsurfaced track on the left takes the route along the top edge of some woods to a path junction above **Twitchill Farm**. You've a choice here. To avoid Win Hill turn left to Twitchill Farm and continue following the route directions in Point 7. To climb to the summit of **Win Hill**, turn right and follow the well-used path up the pasture and then the heathery slopes to the top of the hill. On a clear day there are superb views across this geologically turbulent area where the Dark Peak and White Peak meet as well as the Derbyshire Lake District of the Upper Derwent Valley.

7 From the summit retrace your steps back to the junction above **Twitchill Farm**. This time drop to the farm and walk the driveway to the railway.

8 Turn left under the railway tunnel, where the lane doubles back left and winds its way to **Kilhill Bridge**, then the Edale Road. The **Cheshire Cheese Inn** is 200yds (183m) to the right along here. To return to the centre of **Hope**, however, keep ahead to the village centre crossroads, and turn right to return to the car park.

Cheshire Cheese Inn

The Cheshire Cheese is a real gem, a traditional, unspoilt rural pub and well worth seeking out on this walk. No more than a pair of ivy and creeper-clad stone cottages knocked together, the heart of the building is about 300 years old. A small bar serves three rooms on different levels, all heavily beamed and dimly lit, with lots of brasses, old local photographs and scrubbed pine tables. The small taproom has an old stone fireplace, sturdy cottage-style furnishings and a wealth of old maps and prints on the walls. Relax with pints of hand-pulled local Hartington ale and refuel with some good, home-made bar food. The pub is on the old salt route, and payment for lodging in those days was made in cheese, hence the name.

Food

Choose from the regular printed menu (sandwiches, grilled chicken in leek and Stilton sauce) or look to the blackboard for daily dishes, perhaps home-made fish pie, roast lamb shank in red wine gravy or tuna steak with garlic and tomato sauce.

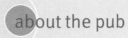

about the pub

Cheshire Cheese Inn
Edale Road, Hope,
Hope Valley, Derbyshire S33 6ZF
Tel 01433 620381

DIRECTIONS: in Hope follow the unclassified lane for Edale, the pub is on left in 0.5 mile (800m)

PARKING: 8

OPEN: daily, all day Saturday and Sunday

FOOD: daily, all day Sunday

BREWERY/COMPANY: free house

REAL ALE: Black Sheep Bitter, Timothy Taylor Landlord, 3 guest beers

DOGS: welcome throughout; water bowls

ROOMS: 3 en suite

Family facilities

Children are welcome inside away from the bar. In addition to a children's menu, smaller portions of the main menu are available. The rear patio has seating and excellent views.

Alternative refreshment stops

The Woodbine Café in Hope.

☛ Where to go from here

The Blue-John Cavern and Mine in Castleton has been a major source of Blue-John stone for nearly 300 years (www.bluejohn-cavern.co.uk).

The Upper Derwent Valley reservoirs

A long and challenging route around the stunning chain of reservoirs in the Upper Derwent Valley.

Birds and bouncing bombs

Many of the high moorlands throughout the northern area of the Peak District are managed for grouse shooting, a long-established practice dating from Victorian times. In today's more conservation-minded days, the gamekeepers employed by the great estates and landowning companies are much more sympathetic to the natural predators of these game birds than were their predecessors.

Nonetheless, birds of prey such as the peregrine falcon are still targetted both by unscrupulous keepers and egg collectors, so defensive measures and management techniques are used to protect such raptors. You may see a peregrine 'stooping' (diving) at up to 150mph to kill its prey on the wing. A much more rare bird of prey is also regaining a toe-hold in the woods around the Upper Derwent reservoirs – the goshawk has recently been reintroduced, and is breeding successfully. During the nesting season (April to June), a remote-controlled camera sends back live pictures of a goshawk nest to the visitor centre at Fairholmes.

Paintings in the Yorkshire Bridge Inn are a reminder that the 617 Dambusters Squadron trained with their bouncing bombs here on Derwent and Howden reservoirs before their remarkable raid on the Ruhr dams in 1943. This was also the location of the film made in 1954 which tells the story of the raid.

the ride

1 Except on summer Sundays, the initial stage of the route is shared with cars, so take care. Head north from the **Fairholmes Centre**, rising to the level of the dam top of Derwent Reservoir. This dam was started in 1902, a year after the dam at Howden. Easy cycling with great views takes you past the memorial to Tip, who was a sheepdog who kept vigil beside his master's body, after the master perished on Howden Moors.

2 Dipping in and out of **Ouzelden Clough**, the road passes close to the site of **Birchinlee**, or 'Tin Town'. This village was created to house the workers who constructed the dams. Most of the buildings were of corrugated iron, hence the nickname. There's little evidence of the place today. Passing beside **Howden Dam**, the route now circuits a long arm of **Howden Reservoir** to arrive at the turning circle at Kings Tree, the end of the tarred road. This is a good place to turn around (9 mile/14.5km round trip) as the next section is more challenging.

3 Beyond the gate the route becomes a rough forest road that climbs gently through the woods above the narrowing tip of Howden Reservoir. At a fork keep right to drop to the old packhorse bridge at **Slippery Stones**. This bridge originally spanned the River Derwent at the hamlet of Derwent, now drowned beneath the waters of Ladybower Reservoir. The structure was rebuilt at this lonely spot on the Howden Moors in the 1940s. Just above the bridge swing sharp right to climb the roughening track along the eastern shore of the reservoir.

Howden Dam

4 The going is pretty rough for a mile (1.6km) or so before a well-graded service road heralds the approach to **Howden Dam**, particularly colourful in late spring and early summer when the rhododendrons are in full flower. A steep, rougher descent follows before the route comes close to the reservoir edge where steep, grassy banks drop straight into the water, so take care here. The track improves considerably as the route nears **Derwent Dam**. Passing close to one of the towers, the way develops into a tarred lane and passes the first of some isolated houses.

5 You can cut short the ride by turning right to pass the foot of **Derwent Dam** to return to **Fairholmes** (9.5 miles/15.2km). The main route continues south past **St Henry's Chapel**, becoming rougher again as it rounds an inlet to an interpretation board describing the now-lost village of Derwent which stood here until the 1940s.

6 Reaching a gateway, join the tarred lane and drop to the main road. Turn right along the wide cycle path across **Ashopton Viaduct,** and right again at the far end.

4h00 | 15 MILES | 24.2 KM | LEVEL 1 2 3

SHORTER ALTERNATIVE ROUTE

2h30 | 9 MILES | 14.5 KM | LEVEL 1 2 3

MAP: OS Explorer OL1 Dark Peak
START/FINISH: Fairholmes Visitor Centre, Upper Derwent Valley, grid ref SK176894
TRAILS/TRACKS: tarred lanes and rough mountain roads
LANDSCAPE: woodland and lakes amidst moorland and craggy valleys
PUBLIC TOILETS: at start
TOURIST INFORMATION: Fairholmes, tel 01433 650953
CYCLE HIRE: Fairholmes, tel 01433 651261
THE PUB: Yorkshire Bridge Inn, Ashopton Road, see Directions to the pub, page 115

ⓘ Take care at the start along a road shared by cars. There are rough tracks on the longer ride. The complete ride is suitable for older family groups using mountain or hybrid-style bikes

Getting to the start
Start at the Fairholmes Visitor Centre in the Upper Derwent Valley. This is signposted off the A57 Glossop to Sheffield road, immediately west of Ashopton Viaduct, which crosses the northern arm of Ladybower Reservoir. Fairholmes is 2 miles (3.2km) along this minor road.

Why do this cycle ride?
This route takes full advantage of the contrasting landscapes of the northern part of the National Park. It's a challenging family route of two halves: a gentle, forested, tarred lane replaced by rough upland tracks.

Researched and written by: Neil Coates

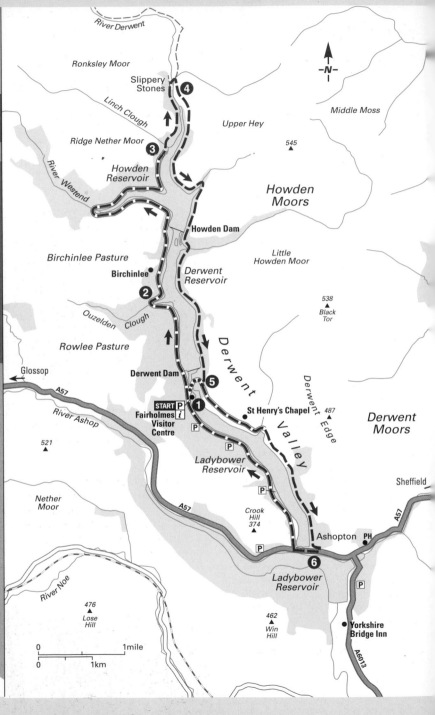

Derwent Valley

DERBYSHIRE

River Derwent

Ronksley Moor

Slippery
Stones
4

Linch Clough

Ridge Nether Moor
3

River Westend

Howden
Reservoir

Upper Hey

Middle Moss

545
▲

Howden
Moors

Howden Dam

Birchinlee Pasture

Birchinlee •
2

Derwent
Reservoir

Little
Howden Moor

Ouzelden Clough

Rowlee Pasture

538
▲
Black
Tor

Glossop
A57

River Ashop

Derwent Dam
5

START P
Fairholmes *i*
Visitor
Centre
1

P

St Henry's Chapel •

Derwent Edge

487
▲

Derwent
Moors

521
▲

P

Nether
Moor

P

Ladybower
Reservoir

Sheffield

A57

A57

Crook
Hill
374
▲

P

Ashopton PH

River Noe

476
▲
Lose
Hill

462
▲
Win
Hill

6

Ladybower
Reservoir

P

Yorkshire
Bridge Inn

A6013

0 ——— 1mile
0 ——— 1km

–N–

Yorkshire Bridge Inn

An armful of awards have been handed out to 'The Bridge' in recent years, not least third place in Pub Garden of the Year. The 200-year-old pub nestles in close to the famous Ladybower Reservoir, scene of the Dambusters' training exercises before their dramatic raid. In summer you'll want to make use of the courtyard and beer garden, while in more inclement weather the bars provide a cosy sanctuary and plenty of interest. Comfortable rooms sport open fires or wood-burning stoves and low beams hung with tankards and jars; one displays photographs of long-lost villages (now under the reservoirs), while another remembers the Dambusters raid.

Food
Food is available in the bar and dining room and starters can range from tandoori chicken strips to giant Yorkshire puddings. Main courses are equally varied with dishes such as chicken italiano, giant prawn cocktail or, from the specials menu, rack of lamb on a minted onion and honey sauce or fresh-dressed crab salad. An impressive selection of sandwiches, filled jacket potatoes and salad platters will more than satisfy those just popping in for a bite.

Family facilities
Children are made very welcome in the bars and the fascinating memorabilia should keep them entertained. On sunny days there's no better place to be than in the beautiful, award-winning gardens. Young children have their own menu and there are cycle racks and secure overnight garaging for guests' use.

about the pub

Yorkshire Bridge Inn
Ashopton Road, Bamford
Hope Valley, Derbyshire S33 0AZ
Tel 01433 651361
www.yorkshire-bridge.co.uk

DIRECTIONS: the Yorkshire Bridge Inn is about 3 miles (4.8km) from the Fairholmes car park. Return to the main road and turn left across the viaduct. At the traffic lights turn right towards Bamford; the pub is 1 mile (1.6km) on the right

PARKING: 60

OPEN: daily, all day

FOOD: daily, all day Sunday

BREWERY/COMPANY: free house

REAL ALE: Timothy Taylor Landlord, Black Sheep Bitter, Stones Bitter, Theakston Old Peculier

ROOMS: 14 en suite

Alternative refreshment stops
There is a snack bar at Fairholmes Visitor Centre and the Ladybower Inn is near Ashopton Viaduct.

☛ Where to go from here
The various caverns at Castleton are a long-time favourite with visitors of all ages. The most unusual is Speedwell Cavern, where access is by an underground boat trip (www.speedwellcavern.co.uk).

Along the Tissington Trail

An easy ride from the Tissington estate village along an old railway line above the secluded valley of the Bletch Brook.

Dew Ponds

Once beyond the old station at Alsop, one feature of the landscape you'll notice along the route are the occasional small ponds in the pastures – these are dew ponds. The name comes from the belief that morning dew would provide sufficient water for cattle and sheep to drink. In days gone by these would be hollows dug out and lined with clay to stop the water from draining away. As this is an area where the rock is predominantly porous limestone, rainwater seeps away and surface water is very rare. The modern-day versions are watertight and they don't rely on dew, either, as they are regularly topped up by the farmers.

Summertime on the Tissington Trail sees a profusion of butterflies. The Common Blue is one of the most noticeable. This very small insect feeds largely on clover flowers and the bright yellow flowers of bird's foot trefoil, a low-growing plant that flourishes in limestone areas. Another butterfly to look out for is the colourful Red Admiral which lays its eggs on nettles, the food plant of the caterpillar.

the ride

1 The Tissington car park is at the site of the old railway station. Take time to find the information board which has a fine picture of the place in its heyday. There's also a village information board here; the village centre is only a short cycle away and it's well worth taking the loop before starting out. Turn left from the car park entrance, then right along **Chapel Lane**. This passes one of the five wells that are dressed in the village during the famous Well Dressing Ceremony held in May on Ascension Day. The lane rises gently to a junction at the top of the village. Turn left to drop down the main street, lined by greens and passing **Tissington Hall** and more wells. At the bottom keep left, passing the village pond before swinging right to return to the car park. Here turn left, passing beneath a bridge to join the old trackbed, which starts a long, easy climb.

2 This initial stretch is through a wooded cutting, soon shallowing to offer the occasional view through the trees across the glorious countryside here at the southern end of the National Park. The panorama sweeps across the peaceful valley of the **Bletch Brook** to take in the high ridge of rough pastures above **Ballidon** to the right.

3 The first natural place to turn around to return to Tissington is the car park and picnic area at the **former Alsop Station**. This would make a round trip of 6 miles (9.7km) and take perhaps 1.5 hours – and it's downhill virtually all the way back!

3h30 · **16 MILES** · **25.7 KM** · **LEVEL 1**23

SHORTER ALTERNATIVE ROUTE

1h30 · **6 MILES** · **9.7 KM** · **LEVEL 1**23

MAP: OS Explorer OL24 White Peak

START/FINISH POINT: Tissington Old Station, grid ref SK 177520

TRAILS/TRACKS: old railway trackbed, lanes in Tissington village

LANDSCAPE: limestone plateau of the White Peak, extensive views

PUBLIC TOILETS: Tissington and Hartington old stations

TOURIST INFORMATION: Ashbourne, tel 01335 343666

CYCLE HIRE: Peak Cycle Hire, Mapleton Lane, Ashbourne, Derbyshire, tel 01335 343156, www.peakdistrict.org

THE PUB: Bluebell Inn, Tissington, see Directions to the pub, page 119

Getting to the start

Tissington is signposted off the A515 Ashbourne to Buxton road, a few miles north of Ashbourne. Pass the pond in the village and bear right to find the gated entrance to the Tissington Trail car park.

Why do this cycle ride?

This is one of England's most famous cycling trails and, as it is an old railway line, you can simply choose just when and where to turn round and return to the start. We've suggested heading north, but you could as easily head south to the pleasant market town of Ashbourne, with its antique shops and bookshops. Going north offers a short option along a wooded route followed by a contrasting, airy route through cuttings and along embankments. It's your choice!

Researched and written by: Neil Coates

4 It's well worth continuing north, however, as once the old railway passes beneath the main road, the character of the Trail changes, and a more open terrain offers different views and experiences. The track continues its gentle climb, soon crossing the first of many embankments. There are grand views left (west) across the rolling pastureland of the **White Peak** towards the higher, darker hills that characterise the Staffordshire moorlands, forming the western horizon. Closer to hand are round-topped hills capped by crowns of trees.

5 Off to your left, the village of **Biggin-by-Hartington** soon appears – notice the old **army huts** down to the left, still put to good use as storerooms. In the distance and looking north, you may pick out the distinctive knolls of limestone near Longnor, Chrome Hill and Parkhouse Hill. The strand of cuttings and embankments continues towards the next logical turning point, **Hartington Old Station**. Here, the former signal box has been preserved; climb the steps to view the old points and levers.

6 This is the ideal place to turn round and retrace the route back to the car park at **Tissington**.

Top: The valley of Bletch Brook

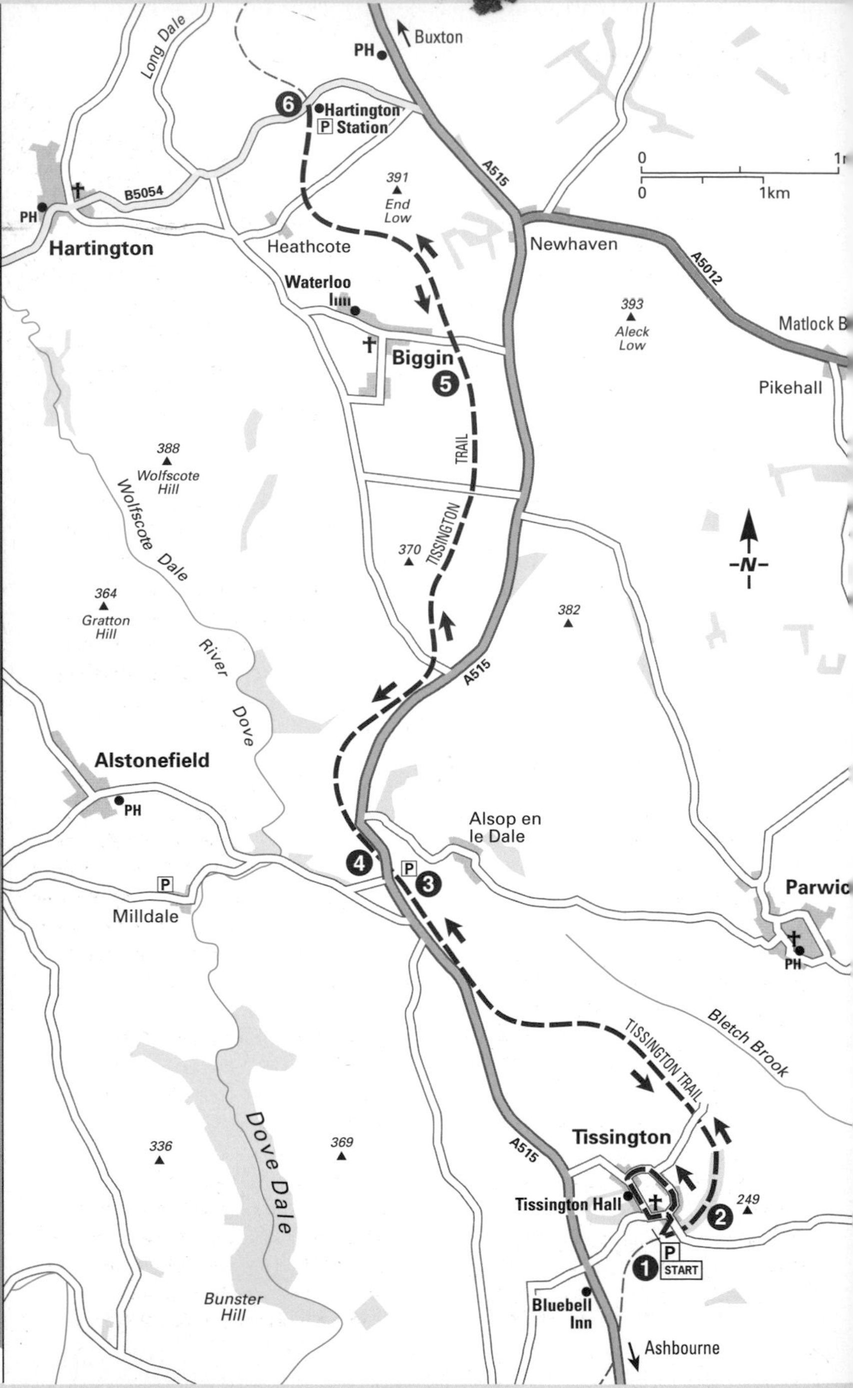

Long Dale

Buxton

PH

6 Hartington
P Station

391
End
Low

B5054

PH

Hartington

Heathcote

Newhaven

A515

A5012

Matlock B

393
Aleck
Low

Waterloo

Biggin

5

Pikehall

388
Wolfscote
Hill

Wolfscote Dale

TRAIL

370

TISSINGTON

-N-

364
Gratton
Hill

River Dove

382

A515

Alstonefield

PH

A515

4

P 3

Alsop en
le Dale

Parwic

PH

Milldale

P

TISSINGTON TRAIL

Bletch Brook

336

369

Dove Dale

A515

Tissington

249

2

Tissington Hall

P
START

1

Bunster
Hill

Bluebell
Inn

Ashbourne

Bluebell Inn

A favourite watering hole for walkers and cyclists following a day on the Tissington Trail, the stone-built Bluebell Inn dates from 1777. In the long, beamed bar you can rest weary legs and savour a reviving pint of Hardys & Hansons bitter. Fires at either end add welcome winter warmth, while in summer vases of flowers on each table add a splash of colour to the narrow room. Prints of local scenes, framed advertisements and old photographs of the pub adorn the walls and high shelves are lined with traditional pub memorabilia. There is a light and airy dining room.

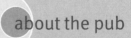

about the pub

Bluebell Inn
Tissington, Ashbourne
Derbyshire DE6 1NH
Tel 01335 350317
www.bluebelltissington.co.uk

DIRECTIONS: from the Tissington Trail car park turn left back through the village to the A515 and turn right to locate the pub beside the main road
PARKING: 75
OPEN: daily, all day March–September
FOOD: daily, all day March–September
BREWERY/COMPANY: Hardys & Hansons Brewery
REAL ALE: Hardys & Hansons Best Bitter and Old Trip

Food

The bar menu is very extensive and lists traditional pub fare. Tuck into wild mushroom lasagne, beef in ale pie, Hartington chicken, a ploughman's lunch or a decent round of sandwiches. Limited daily specials may take in beef and tomato casserole, a giant Yorkshire pudding filled with scrumpy pork casserole, and local trout.

Family facilities

Familes are welcome inside only if they plan to eat. There's a standard selection of children's meals, in addition to portions of lasagne and Yorkshire pudding filled with beef stew. Unfortunately the large garden is next to the busy road so keep an eye on children.

Alternative refreshment stops

There are two village tea rooms in Tissington, the Old Coach House and Bassett Wood Farm.

☞ Where to go from here

Ilam Country Park is a National Trust estate just west of Tissington. Ten miles (16.1km) south of Ashbourne is Sudbury Hall, home to the National Trust's Museum of Childhood (www.nationaltrust.org.uk).

Through Monsal Dale

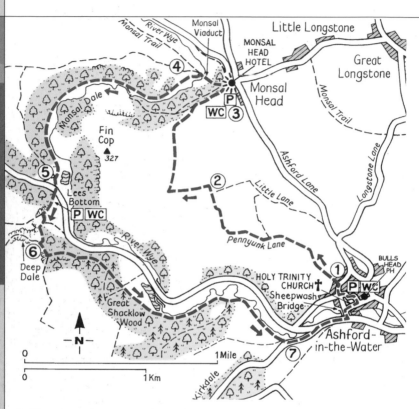

Following the ever-changing River Wye from Ashford-in-the-Water through lovely Monsal Dale.

The Valley of the Gods

The Wye is a chameleon among rivers. Rising as a peaty stream from Axe Edge, it rushes downhill, only to be confined by the concrete and tarmac of Buxton and the quarries to the east. Beyond Chee Dale it gets renewed vigour and cuts a deep gorge through beds of limestone, finally to calm

down again among the gentle fields and hillslopes of Bakewell. The finest stretch of the river valley must be around Monsal Head, and the best approach is that from Ashford-in-the-Water, one of Derbyshire's prettiest villages, just off the busy A6.

After passing through Ashford's streets the route climbs to high pastures that give no clue as to the whereabouts of Monsal Dale. But suddenly you reach the last wall and the ground falls away into a deep wooded gorge. John Ruskin was so taken with this beauty that he likened it to the Vale of Tempe; '...you might have seen the

Gods there morning and evening – Apollo and the sweet Muses of light – walking in fair procession on the lawns of it and to and fro among the pinnacles of its crags'.

It's just a short walk along the rim to reach one of Derbyshire's best-known viewpoints, where the Monsal Viaduct spans the gorge. Built in 1867 as part of the Midland Railway's line to Buxton, the five-arched, stone-built viaduct is nearly 8oft (25m) high. But the building of this railway angered Ruskin. He continued, 'you blasted its rocks away, heaped thousands of tons of shale into its lovely stream. The valley is gone and the Gods with it'.

The line closed in 1968 and the rails were ripped out, leaving only the trackbed and the bridges. Ironically, today's conservationists believe that those are worth saving and have put a conservation order on the viaduct. The trackbed is used as a recreational route for walkers and cyclists – the Monsal Trail. The walk continues over the viaduct, giving birds-eye views of the river and the lawn-like surrounding pastures. It then descends to the riverbank, following it westwards

Hilltop view of Monsal Dale and the disused railway viaduct

3h00 — **5.5 MILES** — **8.8 KM** — **LEVEL 123**

MAP: OS Explorer OL24 White Peak

START/FINISH: Ashford-in-the-Water car park, grid ref SK 194696

PATHS: well-defined paths and tracks throughout, 17 stiles and gates

LANDSCAPE: limestone dales and high pasture

PUBLIC TOILETS: at car park

TOURIST INFORMATION: Bakewell, tel 01629 813227

THE PUB: The Bull's Head, Ashford-in-the-Water, see Getting to the start

🚸 Parents should keep a close eye on children whilst in the vicinity of the Monsal Head Viaduct. There's a short, steady climb in Point 5. Take care crossing the A6

Getting to the start

Ashford-in-the-Water is signposted off the main A6 road a few miles north west of Bakewell. In the village pass the Bull's Head pub on your right and take Court Lane, the next narrow road on the right to the car park.

Researched and written by:
Neil Coates, John Gillham

beneath the prominent peak of Fin Cop. The valley curves like a sickle, while the path weaves in and out of thickets, and by wetlands where tall bulrushes and irises grow. After crossing the A6 the route takes you into the mouth of Deep Dale then the shade of Great Shacklow Wood. Just past some pools filled with trout there's an entrance to the Magpie Mine Sough. The tunnel was built in 1873 to drain the Magpie Lead Mines at nearby Sheldon. Magpie was worked intermittently for over 300 years before finally closing in the 1960s.

the walk

1 From the car park turn right up **Court Lane**, then right again along **Vicarage Lane**. A footpath on the left, signposted '**To Monsal Dale**', doubles back left, then swings sharp right to continue along a ginnel behind a row of houses. Beyond a stile the path enters a field. Head for a stile in the top right corner that drops you into **Pennyunk Lane**, where you turn left. This walled stony track winds among high pastures. Pass by a sign for Monsal Head, continuing to the end of the lane.

2 Turn left here past a squeeze stile and up along a field edge. In 400yds (366m) turn right through two handgates on to another track, heading north towards the rim of **Monsal Dale**. The path runs along the top edge of the deep wooded dale to reach the car park at **Monsal Head**.

3 Take the path marked 'Access to Viaduct' here. Descend steps and walk on to a fingerpost pointing left for '**Viaduct & Monsal Trail**'. Cross the viaduct; at the far end go through a stile on the left and take the middle of three paths, losing height gently through scrub woods down into the valley. This shouldn't be confused with the steep eroded path plummeting straight down to the foot of the viaduct.

what to look for

Ashford's Sheepwash Bridge, over the Wye was built on the original site of the ford that gave the village its name. On the far side of the bridge you can see the enclosures where the sheep were gathered for washing. The square-towered Norman Church of Holy Trinity, has an interesting 'black marble' tympanum over the door.

4 Now you walk down the pleasant valley. The right of way is well away from the river at first but most walkers trace the riverbank to emerge at **Lees Bottom** and a roadside stile.

5 Cross the A6 with care and go through the **White Lodge** car park where the path back to Ashford begins. Pass by the ticket machine and go through the wide gap in the fence and along a surfaced path. Take a stile and remain on the compacted path. At a fork go left; shortly climb a stile at a waymark post for **Ashford**, **Deepdale** and **Sheldon**. A braided path climbs steeply ahead to another low-waymarked fork, here go left for **Ashford** and **Sheldon**. The path continues to rise to a small gateway into **Great Shacklow Wood**.

6 The path now climbs more easily through the trees before levelling out as a ledged path along the steep wooded slopes. Ignore a path signed for Sheldon; eventually the path comes down to the river and shortly passes behind a ruined mill, its wheels still in place. Remain on the path (ignore the bridge) to reach a minor road at the bottom of **Kirkdale**.

7 Turn left along the road, down to the A6 and turn right towards **Ashford**. Leave the road to cross **Sheepwash Bridge**. Turn right along **Church Street**, then left along **Court Lane** to the car park.

The Bull's Head

There's a real buzz about this 17th-century coaching inn tucked away among charming old stone cottages close to the church. Locals in the know fill the place soon after opening, staking their claim to bar stools and favourite tables, as this is the place to eat in Ashford. But it's not just the food that draws folk in. The beamed bars are filled to the brim with antiques, lovely carved settles, cushions, clocks and country prints, and glowing coal fires burn in the grate on cold winter days. Peruse the day's newspapers over a pint of Robinson's Bitter, or tuck into some decent home-cooked food prepared from seasonal ingredients.

Food

You'll find no printed menus or chips here. Daily changing chalkboards may list a dozen dishes, perhaps baked plaice with lobster sauce, salmon and dill fishcakes with lemon sauce, chicken strips in white wine and lovage sauce, and sticky toffee pudding. The excellent lunchtime sandwiches are made with bread baked on the premises.

Feeding the ducks on the River Wye in the Peak District National Park

Family facilities

Children are welcome in the taproom where they can choose small portions of some of the dishes available, but note that this is a chip-free establishment. There is a peaceful rear garden overlooking the village recreation ground.

Alternative refreshment stops

Monsal Head Hotel in Monsal Head serves bar meals.

☛ Where to go from here

At Matlock Farm Park, near Matlock Bath, you'll find British farm animals alongside more exotic breeds. There is also a go-kart track (www.matlockfarmpark.co.uk).

about the pub

The Bull's Head
Church Street, Ashford-in-the-Water
Bakewell, Derbyshire DE45 1QB
Tel 01629 812931

DIRECTIONS: see Getting to the start
PARKING: 12
OPEN: daily
FOOD: no food Thursday evening in winter
BREWERY/COMPANY: Robinson's
REAL ALE: Robinson's Bitter, Old Stockport, seasonal ale
DOGS: welcome inside

Parwich and Tissington

WALK

Joining the famous trackbed Tissington Trail between the differing villages of Parwich and Tissington.

Parwich and Tissington

The approach to Tissington is through a magnificent avenue of lime trees, and when you first see the place it completes the idyll of a perfect village. On one side of a huge green is Tissington Hall, the home of the Fitzherbert family since the reign of Elizabeth I, on the other a neat row of cottages and a slightly elevated Norman church. The trouble with Tissington is that it is too perfect, and to avoid the crowds you'll have to visit mid-week.

On this walk you save Tissington village for last, preferring instead to take to the Tissington Trail, the former trackbed of the Ashbourne-to-Buxton railway, which was closed by Dr Beeching in 1967. The route soon leaves the old track behind and descends into the valley of Bletch Brook, then out again on to a pastured hillside. Now you see Parwich, tucked in the next valley beneath a wooded hill. Overlooking the village is a fine 18th-century red-bricked building, Parwich Hall.

Tissington **DERBYSHIRE**

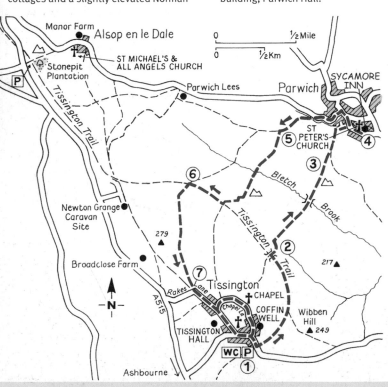

Parwich isn't as grand as Tissington, but it has a village green, and there's a duck pond too. We saw moorhens and their young swimming about among the tangled irises. But Parwich is a more peaceful place and the winding lanes are almost traffic-free in comparison. St Peter's Church is Victorian, but incorporates the chancel arch, and a carved tympanum from the old Norman church.

Leaving Parwich behind, the path continues over the hillside, back into the valley of Bletch Brook and the Tissington Trail, then back for a better look at Tissington. If you go round the lane clockwise you will pass the Methodist chapel before coming to one of Tissington's five wells, the Coffin Well. Every year on Ascension Day Tissington's locals dress these wells. This involves making a clay-covered dressing frame on to which pictures are traced. Flower petals are then pressed into the clay, creating the elaborate patterns and pictures you see. The ceremony is unique to Derbyshire and the Peak District. Originally a pagan ceremony to appease the gods into keeping pure water flowing, it was later adopted

2h30 — **4.25 MILES** — **6.8 KM** — **LEVEL 1** 2 3

MAP: OS Explorer OL24 White Peak

START/FINISH: Tissington, at the Tissington Trail pay car and coach park; grid ref SK 177522

PATHS: field paths, lanes and an old railway trackbed, 28 stiles and gates

LANDSCAPE: village and rolling farm pastures

PUBLIC TOILETS: at car park

TOURIST INFORMATION: Ashbourne, tel 01335 343666

THE PUB: The Sycamore Inn, Parwich, see Point **3** on route

🛈 There are several long, steady climbs which may not be suitable for young children

Getting to the start

Tissington lies just east of the A515, 4 miles (6.4km) north of Buxton. The village car park is at the site of the former railway station, signed as the Tissington Trail Car Park.

Researched and written by:
Neil Coates, John Gillham

View across the village pond to a well-dressing in Tissington

WALK

Tissington

DERBYSHIRE

by the Christian religion. During the Black Death, when people from neighbouring villages were being ravaged by the plague, the Tissington villagers were kept in good health, due, they believe, to the pure water from the five wells. Just past the Coffin Well there's a fine duck pond, complete with a handful of ever-hungry ducks, but most eyes will be on the magnificent Jacobean hall. If it's closed to visitors, you can view it through the fine wrought-iron gates built by Robert Bakewell, or get an elevated view from the churchyard.

the walk

1 From the car park follow the trackbed of the north east bound **Tissington Trail** (the former Ashbourne-to-Buxton railway, which closed in 1967). After about 800yds (732m), at a fingerpost for Tissington and Parwich, leave the trail, rise to and cross the bridge and join a cart track.

2 Just past the first bend descend on the waymarked but trackless path into the valley of **Bletch Brook**, going through several stiles at the field boundaries and across a footbridge spanning the brook itself. A more definite path establishes itself on the climb out of the valley. Beyond a stile beneath a tree keep ahead/right along the field-edge path across the ridge.

3 At a corner, left of a small derelict barn, head downhill in line with the imposing **Parwich Hall** to a squeeze stile and fingerpost. Turn right (**Limestone Way**) and walk to the village playground. The **Sycamore Inn** is on the far side.

4 From the front of the pub turn right and follow the road past the village green. Keep left to a road, left, for **Alsop en le Dale**. Continue to the entrance to **Brook Close Farm**. Take the signed footpath into the

sloping pasture and head for the top-right corner, where a stile leads into another field. At the far top corner of this field a squeeze stile leads to a muddy lane. Turn left to another stile.

5 Turn left and trace the hedge for two fields. Enter a third via an old gateway and aim half right on a path through scrub. Take the footbridge beyond and turn left to another one across **Bletch Brook**. Rise up the middle of the next long field to an old hedge before zig-zagging up to a handgate. Head half right to the bridge over the **Tissington Trail**. Do not cross the bridge, but turn left to gain the trackbed. Turn right to pass beneath the bridge.

6 After 500yds (457m) turn left, following the **Tissington** footpath over a stile to the right-hand corner of a field. Now follow a wall on the right, all the way down to **Rakes Lane** at the edge of Tissington village.

7 Maintain your direction along the lane to reach **Chapel Lane**. You can walk either way round the village square. The hall and church are straight ahead, while the Methodist chapel and the Coffin Well are on Chapel Lane to the left. The car park lies to the south east of the square; take a left turn just beyond the Coffin Well.

what to look for

Many of the regularly ploughed fields of Parwich and Tissington will have few wild flowers in them, but take a look at the field edges and the hayfields, for they will be rich in limestone-loving plants. In April and May, keep a watch for the increasingly rare cowslip (Primula veris). Its short single stem grows from a rosette of wrinkled leaves and its yellow flowers form a drooping cluster that can often be seen swaying in the breeze.

The Sycamore Inn

Rarely do you find a brewery-owned pub that has remained totally unchanged since the 1950s, but Robinson's appear to have forgotten about this tiny gem of a place. The Sycamore is everything a tiny village pub should be – welcoming and friendly, full of lively chat and serving great beer and wholesome food. Off the entrance passageway, the one pocket-sized main bar room has a massive darkwood bar, with old handpumps, framed within huge old reclaimed beams. Around the walls, benches serve a few old tables and there's a brick fireplace with a blazing log fire; the old sash windows look across the brook to the churchyard beyond. There's a separate darts room where families tend to congregate, with an open fire, benches and a few scrubbed pine tables. Outside, you'll find a small, very colourful cottage garden at the front and a few bench tables on a patio overlooking the village play area and pond.

about the pub

The Sycamore Inn
Parwich, Ashbourne
Derbyshire DE6 1QL
Tel 01335 390212

DIRECTIONS: The pub is in the centre of Parwich, which is located off the B5056 between the A5012 and Ashbourne
PARKING: 25
OPEN: daily
FOOD: daily
BREWERY/COMPANY: Robinson's Brewery
REAL ALE: Robinson's Old Stockport, Double Hop, Old Tom and seasonal ales
DOGS: welcome in the bar

Tissington   DERBYSHIRE

Food
Expect hearty home-made soups, good traditional pub dishes like cottage pie, giant Yorkshire pudding filled with minced beef, onions and gravy, mushroom fettucini with salad, garlic and herb butterfly chicken, and a range of steaks, all freshly cooked by the landlady.

Family facilities
The games room is popular with families on cooler days while on fine days the place to be is in the cottage garden or on the patio. Standard children's meals are available.

Alternative refreshment stops
Old Coach House Tearooms in Tissington.

☞ Where to go from here
Near by is Carsington Water with an interactive visitor centre, watersports, mountain bike hire, birdwatching and an extensive events calendar (www.cressbrook.co.uk).

Lathkill Dale

WALK

Lathkill Dale contrasts the wastes of a long-past lead-mining industry with the purity of its water.

Lathkill Dale

DERBYSHIRE

Lead Mining and the Transparent Stream

Today, when you descend the winding lane into this beautiful limestone dale, you're confronted by ash trees growing beneath tiered limestone crags, tumbling screes, multi pastel-coloured grasslands swaying in the breeze and the crystal stream, full of darting trout.

Yet it was not always so. In the 18th and 19th century lead miners came here and stripped the valley of its trees. They drilled shafts and adits into the white rock, built pump houses, elaborate aqueducts, waterwheels and tramways; and when the old schemes failed to realise the intended profits, they came up with new, even bigger ones. Inevitably nobody made any real money, and by 1870 the price of lead had slumped from overseas competition and the pistons finally stopped.

On this walk you will see the fading but still fascinating remnants of this past, juxtaposed with a seemingly natural world that is gradually reclaiming the land. In reality it's English Nature, who are managing the grasslands and woods as part of the Derbyshire Dales National Nature Reserve. The walk starts with a narrow, winding lane from Over Haddon to a clapper bridge by Lathkill Lodge. A lush tangle of semi-aquatic plants surround the river and the valley sides are thick with ash and sycamore. In spring you're likely to see nesting moorhens and mallards. In the

Lathkill Stream flowing through reeds

midst of the trees are some mossy pillars, the remains of an aqueduct built to supply a head of water for the nearby Mandale Mine. The path leaves the woods and the character of the dale changes markedly once again. Here sparse ash trees grow out of the limestone screes, where herb Robert adds splashes of pink.

After climbing out of Cales Dale the walk traverses the high fields of the White Peak plateau. If you haven't already seen them, look out for Jacob's ladder, a 3ft (1m) tall, increasingly rare plant with clusters of bell-like purple-blue flowers. By the time you have crossed the little clapper bridge by Lathkill Lodge and climbed back up that winding lane to the car park, you will have experienced one of Derbyshire's finest dales.

the walk

3h00 · **5 MILES** · **8 KM** · **LEVEL 1 2 3**

1 Turn right out of the car park, and descend the narrow tarmac lane, which winds down into **Lathkill Dale**.

2 Just before reaching **Lathkill Lodge** and the river, turn right along a concessionary track that runs parallel to the north bank. The path passes several caves and a mineshaft as it weaves its way through woodland and thick vegetation. South of **Haddon Grove**, beyond a gate and stile, the trees thin out to reveal the fine limestone crags and screes of the upper dale. The path now is rougher as it traverses an area of screes.

3 Go over the footbridge and follow a little path sneaking into **Cales Dale**. After 400yds (366m) take a left fork along a narrow path down to a stile. You now join the **Limestone Way** long-distance route on a steep, stepped path climbing eastwards out of the dale and on to the high pastures of **Calling Low**.

4 The path heads east of south east across the fields then, just before **Calling Low Farm**, diverts left (waymarked) through several small wooded enclosures. The path swings right beyond the farm, then half left across a pasture to its top left-hand corner and some woods.

5 Over steps in the wall the path cuts a corner through the woods before continuing through more fields to reach a junction of lanes; turn left along the near one.

The old mill in Lathkill Dale

MAP: OS Explorer OL24 White Peak
START/FINISH: Over Haddon pay car park, grid ref SK 203657
PATHS: generally well-defined paths, 24 stiles
LANDSCAPE: partially wooded limestone dales
PUBLIC TOILETS: at car park
TOURIST INFORMATION: Bakewell, tel 01629 813227
THE PUB: Lathkil Hotel, Over Haddon, see Directions to the pub, page 131
🛑 Limestone dale sides can be slippery after rain. The ascent of the steps in Point 3 is particularly long and steep. The climb from the clapper bridge back to Over Haddon at the end of the route is also challenging

Getting to the start

Over Haddon is to the south of the B5055 road that links Bakewell and Monyash. The village is well signposted off this road; the car park is on Main Street.

Researched and written by:
Neil Coates, John Gillham

what to look for

In the dry periods of summer the river may disappear completely under its permeable bed of limestone. The sun-dried soils on the southern slopes are too thin to support the humus-loving plants of the valley bottom. Instead, here you'll see the pretty purple orchid, cowslips with their yellowy primrose-like flowers and clumps of the rock rose with its yellow flowers.

6 After about 500yds (457m), follow a signposted footpath that begins at a stile in a dry-stone wall on the left. This heads north east across fields to the huge farming complex of **Meadow Place Grange**. Waymarks show you the way across the cobbled courtyard, where the path continues between two stable blocks into another field.

7 After heading north across the field to the brow of **Lathkill Dale**, turn right through a gate on to a zig-zag track descending to the river. Cross the old clapper bridge to **Lathkill Lodge** and follow the outward route, a tarmac lane, back to the car park.

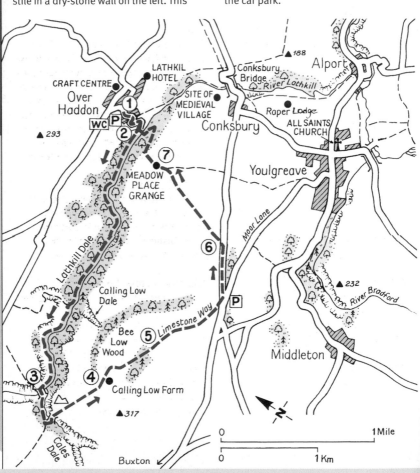

Lathkil Hotel

Formerly 'The Miners Arms', named from the old lead mines that date back to Roman times, an overnight stay at this unpretentious inn remains in the memory for its panoramic views from the Victorian-style bar down into Lathkill Dale and across the village to Youlgreave and Stanton Moor. Much beloved by walkers, who generally fill the two simply furnished rooms at lunchtime, the pub stocks up to five real ales and offers good quality bar meals. The large, airy main bar is warmed by a blazing log fire in winter.

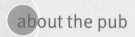

about the pub

Lathkil Hotel
Over Haddon, Bakewell
Derbyshire DE45 1JE
Tel 01629 812501
www.lathkil.co.uk

DIRECTIONS: 400yds (366m) from the village car park, along Main Street, then Wellgate Lane	
PARKING: roadside parking	
OPEN: daily, all day Saturday and Sunday	
FOOD: daily	
BREWERY/COMPANY: free house	
REAL ALE: Marston's Pedigree, Hartington Bitter, guest beers	
DOGS: welcome in the bar	
ROOMS: 4 en suite	

Food
The home-cooked food has an enviable reputation locally with a lunchtime hot and cold buffet in summer and more extensive evening choices supplemented by cooked-to-order pizzas. Typically, tuck into tiger prawns in filo pastry, then follow with sea bass with garlic and rosemary or Wootton Farm venison steak with Stilton sauce. Good soups and filled rolls at lunchtime.

Family facilities
Children are welcome in the dining room where they have a children's menu to choose from. Smaller portions of main menu dishes are also available. There is patio seating with wonderful views.

Alternative refreshment stops
Geoff's Diner or the café in the craft centre.

☞ Where to go from here
Nearby Haddon Hall, home of the Dukes of Rutland, is well worth a visit. This impressive 14th-century country house has beautifully laid out gardens surrounding a Gothic style main building (www.haddonhall.co.uk).

Lathkill Dale

DERBYSHIRE

Osmaston and Shirley

CYCLE

Follow challenging gravel roads and peaceful back lanes between charming medieval and estate villages near Ashbourne.

Shirley village

Shirley is the oldest of a gaggle of peaceful little villages visited on this ride. The village is recorded in the Domesday book; St Michael's Church originates from this period although it was rebuilt in Victorian times when the renowned Edwardian novelists, brothers John Cowper and Theodore Francis Powys, were born in the vicarage here. Note the enormous yew tree in the churchyard. At the edge of the village is Shirley Hall, family home to the Earls Ferrers.

The valley of Shirley Brook was dammed to power mills, of which the most spectacular is the glorious Osmaston Saw Mill. This is on your left at the foot of the first long, rough descent. The vast,

landscaped lake powered the overshot wheel that still survives beneath its imposing gable. The mill itself is a rather eccentric building built in 1845 for the owners of Osmaston Hall. The cedar-tree dotted parkland still contains the walled gardens, but the hall itself is no more. Osmaston village, built largely to house workers on the estate, is a charming mix of thatched cottages and picturesque houses and farms surrounding a village duck pond.

the ride

1 Ride uphill from the **Saracen's Head**, shortly passing by the gates to **St Michael's Church** at the heart of the village of Shirley. At the bend, fork left along the level lane, singposted '**No Through Road**'. This starts a very gradual climb away from the village. Beyond the sports ground, the lane becomes a rough track.

2 Keep left at the fork by the **brick barn**, starting a hill which courses along the

Shirley

DERBYSHIRE

edge of a largely fir tree plantation. At the top a cross-track runs along the lip of a steep slope. Go ahead here down a very steep and loose gravel descent through beech woods into the valley of **Shirley Brook**. It levels off between a huge mill pond and the old **saw mill**, before commencing an equally challenging ascent through landscaped **Osmaston Park**. Keep ahead as the surface changes to tar and then back again, before reaching the valley crest above a spinney. Ride ahead from here to reach the village of **Osmaston**.

3 It's worth exploring this charming little village before returning to the duck pond and green. Put this on your left and take the road for **Wyaston** and **Yeaveley**. A level 0.5 miles (800m) follows, the typical higher hedges with banks of wild flowers lining the route. A descent into a shallow valley means a lengthy uphill stretch before the quiet, winding lane reaches the **Shire Horse Inn** at the edge of **Wyaston**. Keep on the main lane, soon entering this straggling hamlet. Pass by the first left turn and continue beyond the village to a second left turn (Shirley and Rodsley), also signed as **National Cycle Trail 68**. Turn left here and trace the lane all the way through to the cross lanes at the heart of **Rodsley**.

4 You have a choice of routes here. To cut the full route short, turn left at this crossroads and cycle the lane back to Shirley. It's an undulating lane with a long but gradual hill after **Shirley Mill Farm** as the final flourish into **Shirley** itself. For the

Top: Village green pond in Osmaston
Left: Osmaston Saw Mill

3h30 · **10 MILES** · **16.1 KM** · **LEVEL 2**

SHORTER ALTERNATIVE ROUTE

2h30 · **6.75 MILES** · **10.9 KM** · **LEVEL 2**

MAP: OS Explorer 259 Derby
START/FINISH: Saracen's Head in Shirley (check with landlord beforehand for parking), grid ref SK 220416
TRAILS/TRACKS: back lanes and rough tracks, one section of busier road on the longer option
LANDSCAPE: mixed arable and pasture farmland, country estates
PUBLIC TOILETS: none on route
TOURIST INFORMATION: Ashbourne, tel 01335 343666
CYCLE HIRE: nearest is on the Tissington Trail at Mapleton Lane, north of Ashbourne town centre, tel 01335 343156
THE PUB: The Saracen's Head, Shirley, see Point **1** on route

🚴 Some short, steep ascents and descents; high hedges along some roads. Some very challenging short hills, which will not suit younger children or less-fit cyclists. The longer option has a section of busier road, with good sight lines. Suitable for experienced family groups with older children who have some road cycling experience

Getting to the start
Shirley is signposted off the A52 about 6 miles (9.6km) south east of Ashbourne.

Why do this cycle ride?
A web of quiet by-roads and single track lanes threads this peaceful area. The result is rewarding cycling amidst hay meadows, pastureland, woods and fields, with good views, and visits to several estate villages.

Researched and written by: Neil Coates

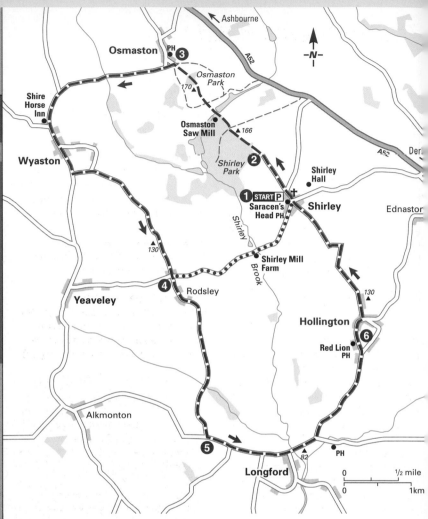

longer route, keep ahead at the crossroads, rising up through the hamlet along a narrowing lane to trace a winding course through to a T-junction with a busier road.

5 Turn left here along **Long Lane**. The road is easy riding, but take care as traffic is faster and much more common. Great views open out across south Derbyshire as you drop gradually into the valley of **Longford Brook**. In a mile (1.6km) turn left at a sign for

Hollington, starting a gradual climb up **Hoargate Lane**. At a junction with Back Lane, keep left up along **Main Street** and past the strand of houses and farms of **Hollington**.

6 Pass by the **Red Lion** and bend right to reach a cross lanes. Turn left along **Shirley Lane** (also Marsh Hollow), following this single track, partially green-centred lane through to **Shirley** village.

The Saracen's Head

Pub and church stand close together at the heart of this tiny, picturesque village. The pub (dated 1791) is an attractive white-painted brick building, with plants clambering up the walls and a tiny front garden filled with delphiniums. To the rear, outbuildings have been converted into letting cottages. Inside you'll find a single, L-shaped bar with a mix of tiled and carpeted floors, comfortable upholstered bench seating, and lovely views of rose-bedecked cottages and the churchyard. On tap you'll find a decent pint of Black Sheep Bitter and the menu lists some good, home-cooked food. A great village pub with few pretensions, an affable landlord and an easy-going atmosphere.

Food

The bar menu offers a good choice of home-cooked food, for example game pie, haddock and chips, steak and kidney pie, chicken, bacon and mushroom pie and decent filled rolls. Blackboard specials

might highlight a range of curries including Thai green chicken.

Family facilities

Small children have a standard menu to select from. They can tuck into their meal in the pub or on fine days they can enjoy the flower-filled garden and the village views.

Alternative refreshment stops

Pubs at Osmaston (Shoulder of Mutton) and Wyaston (The Shire Horse).

☞ Where to go from here

Kedleston Hall is one of England's greatest country houses, built in 1765 when the entire village was moved to improve the owner's views (www.nationaltrust.org.uk).

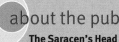

about the pub

The Saracen's Head
Shirley, Ashbourne
Derbyshire DE6 3AS
Tel 01335 360330

DIRECTIONS: see Getting to the start
PARKING: 20. Please check beforehand with landlord before leaving your car in the car park
OPEN: closed Sunday evenings and all day Monday
FOOD: daily
BREWERY/COMPANY: free house
REAL ALE: Black Sheep Bitter, Bass, Marston's Pedigree
ROOMS: 1 en suite

Bakewell and the Monsal Trail

CYCLE

An easy ride from the town of Bakewell, with its railway heritage, which loops through a picturesque limestone village and riverside hay meadows.

Bakewell and the Monsal Trail

The Monsal Trail is largely the trackbed of the former main line railway linking Manchester Central to Derby and London St Pancras. Opened in 1849 and built by the Midland Railway, it was latterly renowned for its comfortable Pullman carriages before closing in 1969. There

Bakewell is famed for its puddings, but there's much more to look out for here, including the Old House Museum and the lively market (Wednesdays are particularly busy and vibrant). Great Longstone was once a renowned centre for stocking manufacture, established by immigrant Flemish weavers who often traded their goods at the village market cross.

the ride

1 Access to the trackbed remains via the gap at the left side of the imposing structure. Turn left along the level track, a compacted and well-surfaced route that, beyond the industrial units that occupy the

are ambitious plans to restore services through the Peak District, and a start has been made at nearby Rowsley, from where Peak Rail runs seasonal services through to Matlock and the surviving branch line to Derby. During the summer months the railway's banks (and the roadside verges) are bright with the vivid blue flower of the meadow cranesbill, that can often be seen in great drifts along with the ox-eye daisies and willowherb.

former goods yard, runs initially through thin woods. Passing beneath the main road, the buildings of Bakewell are left behind and soon **Hassop Old Station** comes into view.

2 The station buildings are largely gone, although an old warehouse has been converted to other uses. Beyond here, the trees become less constricting, and views to the hill slopes climbing towards **Longstone Edge** draw the eye. There's an

Right: A medieval cross on the small green of the limestone-built village of Great Longstone

3h00	8 MILES	12.9 KM	LEVEL 1 2 3

SHORTER ALTERNATIVE ROUTE

1h15	5.25 MILES	8.4 KM	LEVEL 1 2 3

MAP: OS Explorer OL24 White Peak

START/FINISH: Bakewell Old Station, grid ref SK223690

TRAILS/TRACKS: old railway trackbed and back lanes

LANDSCAPE: woods and pastures below limestone edges, river valley, hay meadows

PUBLIC TOILETS: central Bakewell

TOURIST INFORMATION: Bakewell, tel 01629 813227

CYCLE HIRE: none near by

THE PUB: Monsal Head Hotel, Monsal Head, see Directions to the pub, page 139

❶ One short climb, one long downhill stretch

Getting to the start

The old railway station in Bakewell is located on Station Road – the road that forks off to the right at the memorial as you take the A619 road for Baslow out of the town centre and cross the bridge over the Wye. There's ample parking at the old station.

Why do this cycle ride?

This is an easy, largely level ride from Bakewell into the folded, wooded countryside that characterises the eastern fringes of the national park. A couple of shorter add-ons include one of the Peak's charming little villages and a pleasant ride above the Wye Valley.

Researched and written by: Neil Coates

abundance of summer wild flowers along this section. The old trackbed passes under and over several roads and lanes before reaching the impressive buildings at Great Longstone's **old station**. The station partially retains its canopy, while next door is one of the buildings of the Thornbridge Estate.

3 A sign here warns that there is no exit for cycles beyond this point, but it is worth cycling the extra .25 mile (400m) to the end of the useable track for some great views across towards the hidden **River Wye** in its deep valley. You can choose here to simply retrace your route back to Bakewell, a total distance of 5.25 miles (8.4km). Another option, though, is to return to **Great Longstone Station** and take the steep flight of steps, left, to a minor road. Turn left along this, an easy, level ride to the village centre at **Great Longstone**.

4 At the market cross and village green, fork right along either of the lanes. Both wind down to the main street, lined with fine limestone cottages and houses, to reach the White Lion. Just beyond this, take **Church Lane**, left, to rise up a gentle hill to the parish **church**. The road bends right here, commencing an undulating, easy ride along this narrow road, **Beggarway Lane**, offering excellent views up to **Longstone Edge** and occasional glimpses back towards Bakewell.

5 In about 0.75 miles (1.2km), turn right along the lane that leaves at a left bend. This, **Longreave Lane**, is an easy downhill

Left: Medieval five-arch bridge spanning the River Wye in Bakewell

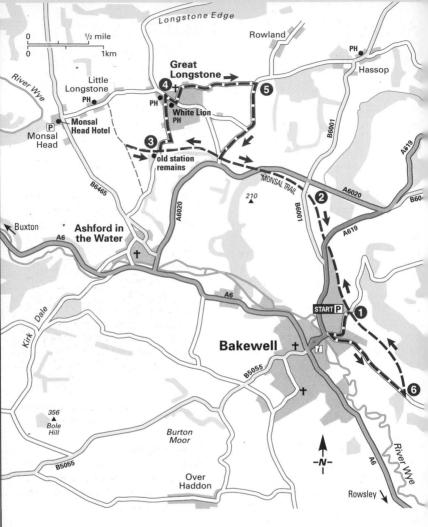

coast for nearly a mile (1.6km), eventually reaching a junction at a railway overbridge. Fork left here just before the bridge, up a gravelly ramp to regain the old railway. Turn left to return to **Bakewell**. To extend the route you can now cycle across the car park and take **Station Road** downhill (take care by the parked cars). At the junction at the bottom turn sharp left along **Coombs Road**, passing the car park entrance. This peaceful, level lane runs for about

a mile (1.6km), amid pastures and hay meadows to reach a high-arched viaduct crossing.

6 Immediately before the viaduct, look for the **Monsal Trail** board on the left, indicating a short, sharp incline up which you wheel your bicycle to gain the old railway. Turn left to return to **Bakewell**; there are some good views across the town from this elevated route.

Monsal Head Hotel

Set against a spectacular backdrop of hills and dales, the disused viaduct at Monsal Head has long been a familiar landmark in the Peak District. In days gone by horses pulled guests and their luggage from the railway station up the steep incline to this imposing, ivy-covered hotel. However, the place for walkers, cyclists and passing trade is the Stables Pub to the rear of the building. The former stables, converted into a thriving bar, offer real ale and great food. Outside it's bare stone, two storeys with a steep pitched roof and wooden sash windows, while inside the fittings have been largely retained, with half-a-dozen stalls converted into individual drinking corners, each with cushioned wall benches. Add a huge solid fuel stove for cold winter days, eight real ales on handpump and a super courtyard garden for summer drinking and you have a great pub to retreat to after your ride.

Food

One menu operates throughout the restaurant, bar and eating area, with specials such as char-grilled wild boar, braised ham shank, and roast chump of lamb, as well as halibut, monkfish, salmon and scallops from a good fishy choice.

about the pub

Monsal Head Hotel
Monsal Head, Bakewell
Derbyshire DE45 1NL
Tel 01629 640250
www.monsalhead.com

DIRECTIONS: from Bakewell Old Station drop to the main road junction and turn right for Baslow. In 0.5 miles (800m) fork left (B6001) and continue to a traffic island. Turn left, then right after a mile (1.6km) to Great Longstone. Continue through the village to Monsal Head

PARKING: 15 (pay car park adjacent)

OPEN: daily, all day

FOOD: daily, all day

BREWERY/COMPANY: free house

REAL ALE: Caledonian Deuchars IPA, Theakston Best and Old Peculiar, Timothy Taylor Landlord, local guest beers

ROOMS: 8 en suite

Small plates, grills, salads, omelettes and jacket potatoes extend the range.

Family facilities

Children are welcome away from the bar and small children have their own menu. There's good courtyard seating with plenty of tables and chairs.

Alternative refreshment stops

Pubs in Great Longstone (The Crispin Inn and The White Lion); plenty of choice in Bakewell.

☞ Where to go from here

The Peak Rail preserved railway (south of Rowsley) runs seasonal services, mostly steam operated (www.peakrail.co.uk). The spectacular medieval fortified manor of Haddon Hall has featured in many films and TV programmes (www.haddonhall.co.uk).

Around Carsington Water

Discover picturesque hamlets and abundant wildlife at one of England's largest reservoirs.

The Reservoir

Carsington Water, at the heart of the route, was opened in 1992 and is one of the largest reservoirs in England. The visitor centre tells the story of the reservoir and

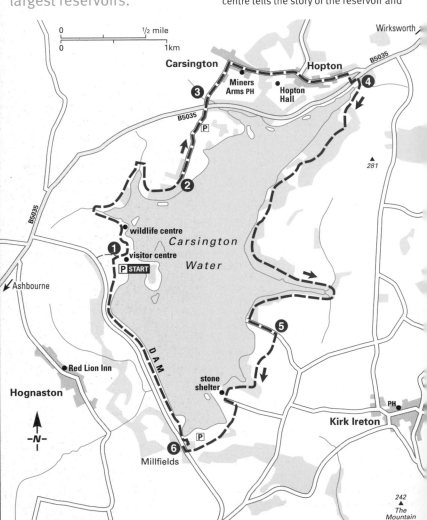

Left: Carving beside the trail around Carsington Water

3h30 · **8 MILES** · **12.9 KM** · **LEVEL 1 2 3**

the surrounding area in a display aimed largely at children who visit on school trips. The reservoir covers an area of 741 acres (300ha) and is just over 100ft (30m) at its deepest. Its location, high up above major river catchments and close to limestone uplands (although the site itself is on impermeable sandstones and shales), means that most of its water is pumped up from the River Derwent at Ambergate, which is over 6 miles (9.7km) away and is 430ft (131m) lower than the average water level in the reservoir.

It is part of a complex, interlinked series of reservoirs and aqueducts that include the massive series of lakes in the upper Derwent Valley to the west of Sheffield, supplying water to domestic and industrial consumers in places as far apart as Derby, Nottingham and Leicester. There are rowing boats for hire and, a short walk from the visitor centre, there is a Wildlife Centre with a well-equipped bird hide and displays explaining the conservation measures adopted here.

MAP: OS Explorer OL24 White Peak
START/FINISH: Carsington Reservoir Visitor Centre, grid ref SK241515
TRAILS/TRACKS: largely compacted gravel, sand and earth tracks, with some back lanes
LANDSCAPE: woodland and waterside
PUBLIC TOILETS: at the start and the Millfields parking area at Point 6 of the route
TOURIST INFORMATION: Ashbourne, tel 01335 343666
CYCLE HIRE: The Watersports Centre, Carsington Water, tel 01629 540478
THE PUB: Red Lion Inn, Main Street, Hognaston, see Directions to the pub page 143
🛈 Some short, steep climbs and a couple of longer ascents through woodland

Getting to the start

Carsington Water is signed from the B5035 between Ashbourne and Wirksworth. The route starts at the visitor centre on the western shore of the reservoir

Why do this cycle ride?

This is an enjoyable circuit with a mix of level tracks, a section of road cycling on back lanes through the picturesque hamlets of Carsington and Hopton, and with more challenging ascents and descents on the eastern side of the reservoir.

Researched and written by: Neil Coates

the ride

1 From the car park at the **visitor centre** look for the fingerposts pointing the way to the **wildlife centre**; this will bring you to the start of a sandy, compacted track just below the coach park. These initial stages are an easy settling in section, with a few short hills and descents, largely between hedges and offering occasional glimpses of the reservoir. The track is partly shared with walkers and partly designated as a horse and cycle route, so be prepared to stop and obey any instruction signs.

2 The track joins a tarred farm access road, shortly passing by the **Sheepwash** car park. Take extra care here as you join the car park access road before arriving at the main road. The way is diagonally across to the left and along the minor road for Carsington.

3 There's a steady climb before the lane descends into **Carsington**, a picturesque village of old limestone cottages and houses. The local inn, the **Miners Arms**, recalls that the area was once a thriving mining community – lead ore was the staple raw material extracted hereabouts. The lane undulates gently through the village and the neighbouring hamlet of Hopton. Pass beside the remarkable wall surrounding the **Hopton Hall Estate**, a wavy barrier of bricks with square towers and rounded bays. At the far end of Hopton, pass by **Henmore Grange** before looking right for the waymarked, fenced path that drops steeply down to a gate on to the B5035.

4 Cross carefully here, go left signed for **Millfields**, and turn right along the track beyond a further safety gate. You're at the

extremity of the reservoir here, with views down the length of the lake. The first of a long series of hills is soon encountered, leading to a gate into woodlands with a wealth of wild flowers, and many short descents and longer inclines. You rise high above the waterline here before cresting a final summit to reveal views towards the dam and valve tower, and a steep hill down, passing by a wooden carving, just one of the sculptures dotted around the reservoir. When you eventually reach a short section of tarred farm lane, turn up along this to a waymarked gate, right, back on to the track.

5 Further ups and downs bring you past a **stone shelter**; take a peek inside to find some inventive wooden carvings. Just past here turn up the old lane. Pass by the farmhouse before looking right for the waymarked gateway back on to the cycle track. From here you're once again on a dedicated cycle/horse track that brings you to a gateway on to a wide grass verge by the main road. Turn right down the verge and right again into **Millfields**.

6 The waymarking is confusing here. Take the marked cycle path past the entry barriers and then go sharp left along a track. Go round a bend and along a short straight section, then dogleg left then right along a sandy track to reach the dam. At the far end head back to the **visitor centre**.

The Visitor Centre at Carsington Water

Red Lion Inn

Standing next to the squat medieval parish church, the 17th-century Red Lion is a charming traditional village inn. Expect a mix of floorboards and quarry tile flooring, a huge old stone fireplace, a carved and panelled wood bar, some exposed stone walls, and antique furnishings amidst time-worn old pub and farmhouse tables and chairs in the cosy, L-shaped main bar. In the upper bar room you'll find worn settles, old chapel chairs still with their prayer-book racks, a grandfather clock and another blazing log fire. Here you'll find bric-a-brac, country prints and old photos, while to the rear the conservatory restaurant (same menus) is altogether lighter and more modern, with colourful prints, potted plants and more contemporary furniture. There is a welcoming atmosphere throughout.

Food

From an imaginative chalkboard menu, order starters of home-made soup with warm bread or calamari with sweet chilli dipping sauce, or tuck into roast leg of lamb with redcurrant gravy and apricot and hazelnut stuffing, or whole sea bass with prawns and a Pernod and chive sauce.

Family facilities

Children are welcome inside the bar if they are eating and smaller portions of the main menu are available. There is summer seating to the front of the pub.

Alternative refreshment stops

The Miner's Arms at Carsington; a restaurant and café at the reservoir visitor centre.

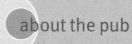

about the pub

Red Lion Inn
Main Street, Hognaston
Ashbourne, Derbyshire DE6 1PR
Tel 01335 370396
www.lionrouge.com

DIRECTIONS: The Red Lion in Hognaston, is about 1.5 miles (2.4km) from the visitor centre. Load the bikes on to the car, then turn right at the car park entrance to reach a T-junction with the B5035. Turn left, then left again signposted 'Hognaston Only'. The pub is on the left next to the church

PARKING: 25

OPEN: closed Monday

FOOD: no food Sunday evening

BREWERY/COMPANY: free house

REAL ALE: Marston's Pedigree, Bass, Greene King Old Speckled Hen, Hartington Bitter

ROOMS: 3 en suite

☛ Where to go from here

Ten miles (16.1km) east of Carsington is Heage Windmill (grid ref 367507) a squat stone tower built of local sandstone, with six sails (www.heagewindmill.co.uk).

Stanage Edge

WALK

Skirting the gritstone cliffs
which line Sheffield's
moorland edge.

Above: View south east along Stanage Edge
Below right: Grave of Little John

Hathersage and Stanage

From Moscar to Baslow a line of dark
dramatic cliffs cap the heather moors east
of the Derwent Valley. Stanage Edge, the
highest of these cliffs, is a great place for
walkers, to stride out on firm skyline paths
with Yorkshire on one side and Derbyshire
on the other. High car parks mean that you
can walk Stanage without much ascent, but
it's more rewarding to work for your fun, so
we'll start the route at Hathersage.

Hathersage is a neat village by the
banks of the Derwent. The route starts on
Baulk Lane and passes the cricket ground
on its way through the little valley of Hood
Brook. Gradients steepen and the route
comes across the 16th-century castellated
manor of North Lees Hall, the inspiration for
Thornfield Hall, Mr Rochester's home in
Jane Eyre. The remains of a chapel, built in
1685, only to be destroyed three years later,
can still be seen in the grounds.

Above the hall the route climbs on to
the moors and a paved causey track known
as Jacob's Ladder takes it to the top of the
cliffs. The cliff-edge path to High Neb and
Crow Chin is a delight, the extensive views
taking in a good deal of the Derwent and
Hope valleys, Mam Tor and Kinder Scout. It
may seem strange to descend to the foot of
the cliffs, but the lost height doesn't
amount to much and you can now view
them from the perspective of the climber.

After rejoining the edge, the path
passes above Robin Hood's Cave, where
the legendary outlaw perhaps hid from the

Sheriff of Nottingham, to reach the high
road and climbers' car park. Now there's
just Higger Tor to do. The rocky knoll
surrounded by an ocean of heather makes a
fine finale, one last lofty perch before the
descent back to Hathersage.

the walk

1 From the car park in **Hathersage**,
head up **Oddfellows Road** past the
fire station. At the bend, go ahead into
Ibbotsons Croft and along the ginnel
through to the main road. Virtually
opposite, to the right of **The Square**, join
Baulk Lane. This soon passes the cricket
ground. Beyond houses it becomes an
unsurfaced track.

2 Just short of **Cowclose Farm** take the
signposted left fork, which passes to
the right of **Brookfield Manor** to reach
Birley Lane. Turn right here, then left along
a drive to **North Lees Hall**. After rounding
the hall, turn right, climbing some steps
that cut the corner to another track. This
crosses hillside pastures before continuing
through attractive mixed woodland.

3 A stepped path on the left makes a
short cut to a roadside toilet block and
mountain rescue post. Opposite this, a

grassy path heads for the rocks of **Stanage Edge**. After 200yds (183m) you join the path from the nearby car park. A paved path now climbs through **Stanage Plantation** before arcing left to the cliff top.

4 For the shorter option, turn right along the edge and pick up the route as detailed in Point 5, below. For the longer walk option, follow the firm edge path north westwards (left) to see the summit of **High Neb** and **Crow Chin**.

5 When you reach **Crow Chin**, where the edge veers north 200yds (183m) beyond the trig pillar, descend to a lower path that doubles back beneath the cliffs. Keeping within 100yds (91m) or so of the cliffs, this eventually joins a track coming up from the right, which returns the route to the top of the cliffs. (Shorter option continues from here). Continue walking south east along the edge, soon keeping a broken wall on your left to eventually reach the trig pillar on the bouldery east summit (marked on OS maps by a spot height of 457m).

6 The track continues to the road at **Upper Burbage Bridge**. Go left along the road for 100yds (91m), then turn right to take the higher of the two paths from the rear of the parking area before the bridges which head south to the top of **Higger Tor**.

7 From the rocky top, double back on a side path to the **Fiddler's Elbow Road** and two stiles opposite each other. Cross these and walk 30 paces to a wide cross-track. Turn left on this, and descend to **Callow Bank** to a walled track leading down to the **Dale Bottom Road**. Follow the road

4h30 — **9 MILES** — **14.5 KM** — **LEVEL 1 2 3**

SHORTER ALTERNATIVE ROUTE

3h00 — **5.75 MILES** — **9.2 KM** — **LEVEL 1 2 3**

MAP: OS Explorer OL1 Dark Peak

START/FINISH: Hathersage car park, grid ref SK 232814

PATHS: well-defined paths and tracks, about 16 stiles and gates

LANDSCAPE: gritstone and heather moorland

PUBLIC TOILETS: at car park and on lane above North Lees

TOURIST INFORMATION: Castleton, tel 01433 620679

THE PUB: The Scotsman's Pack, Hathersage, see Point 8 on route

🛈 Do not attempt this walk in misty weather. It is a very long, rewarding walk suitable for experienced family groups

Getting to the start

Hathersage is on the A6187 Hope Valley road. From Sheffield take the A625 and turn off right at the signs to Hope, Castleton and various caves. The pay car park in Hathersage is near the swimming pool and is signposted off the main street along Station Road (B6001).

Researched and written by:
Neil Coates, John Gillham

down for 300yds (274m) to a track on the right that traverses the hillslopes to **Toothill Farm**. Turn sharp left before the farmhouse on to a gated track that becomes a grassy field road. In 300yds (274m) look right for a stile into a sunken path leading to a tarred lane, taking the route through housing and down to Hathersage's impressively spired church and the Roman fort of **Camp Green**.

8 Turn right down **School Lane**, past the **Scotsman's Pack**, to reach **Main Road**, which descends into the centre of **Hathersage**. Then go left up the ginnel

what to look for

Beneath the cliffs of Stanage Edge you'll see piles of old millstones and grindstones, some intact and some incomplete. They are the abandoned relics of an industry that supplied the flourishing steelworks of Sheffield and local corn mills. French imports, which were both cheaper and better, and the coming of the roller mills saw the decline of the industry by the 1860s.

opposite **The Square** to return to the car park at **Hathersage**.

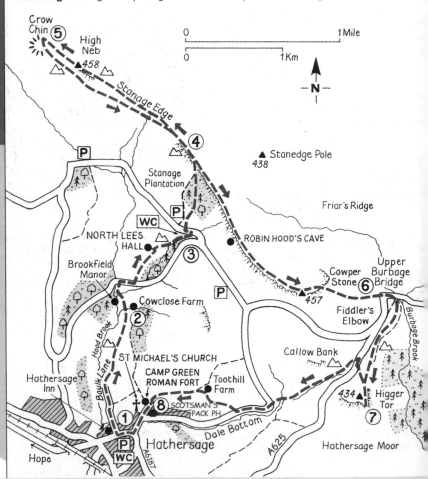

The Scotsman's Pack

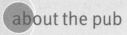

Set into a hillside at the eastern edge of Hathersage, this imposing, gabled Edwardian inn borders a rushing trout stream and has long been a favoured watering hole among the local walking fraternity. The interior resembles a 'gentleman's parlour', with wood panelling and a huge copper fireplace at one end. The decorative beams are festooned with gleaming horsebrasses, and country prints and plates adorn the walls and display dressers. Comfortable wall-bench seating and an assortment of tables and darkwood chairs top the red carpet throughout the open-plan bar. Plush and modern it may be, but the welcome is warm and the huge selection of food is very popular.

Food

Main menu dishes include smoked fish medley, pan-fried lambs' liver with bacon, and pork steak with apricot and ginger sauce. Daily specials may take in rack of lamb with mint gravy, beef fillet with Roquefort and brandy sauce, and a good selection of vegetarian meals. Book for Sunday lunch.

about the pub

The Scotsman's Pack
School Lane, Hathersage
Hope Valley, Derbyshire S32 1BZ
Tel 01433 650253

DIRECTIONS: at the eastern edge of Hathersage on Point 8 of the route – see Getting to the start
PARKING: 14
OPEN: daily, all day Saturday and Sunday
FOOD: daily, all day Saturday and Sunday
BREWERY/COMPANY: Burtonwood
REAL ALE: Burtonwood Bitter and Top Hat, guest beer
DOGS: not allowed inside
ROOMS: 5 en suite

Family facilities

Well-behaved children are allowed in, if eating, at lunchtimes and early evenings. There is sheltered patio seating above the stream.

Alternative refreshment stops

There's generally a snack van on the car park at Upper Burbage Bridge.

☛ Where to go from here

See how everyday knives, forks, spoons and other tableware are made at the David Mellor Cutlery Factory at The Round Building just south of Hathersage off the B6001 (www.davidmellordesign.co.uk).

WALK

Bradfield and the Dale Dike Reservoir

A quiet waterside walk around reservoirs and through woods.

The Bradfield Scheme

Just before midnight on Friday 11 March 1864, the Dale Dike Dam collapsed, sending 650 million gallons (2,955 million litres) of water surging along the Loxley Valley towards Sheffield, leaving a trail of death and destruction. When the floods finally subsided 244 people had been killed and hundreds of properties destroyed.

During the Industrial Revolution Sheffield expanded rapidly, as country

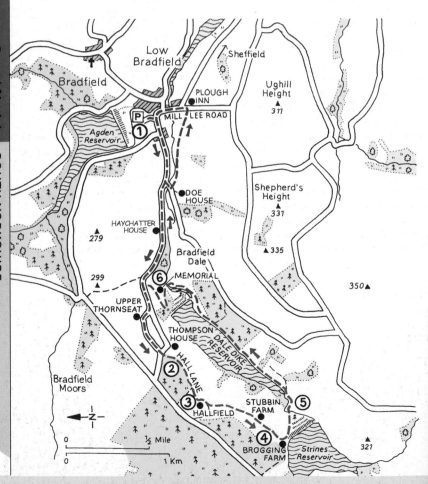

people sought employment in the city's steel and cutlery works. This put considerable pressure on the water supply. The 'Bradfield Scheme' was Sheffield Waterworks Company's proposal to build massive reservoirs in the hills around the village of Bradfield, about 8 miles (12.9km) from the city. Work commenced on the first of these, the Dale Dike Dam on 1 January 1859. It was a giant by the standards of the time with a capacity of over 700 million gallons (3,182 million litres) of water, but some 200 million gallons (910 million litres) less than the present reservoir.

Construction of the dam continued until late February 1864, by which time the reservoir was almost full. Friday 11 March was a stormy day and as one of the dam workers crossed the earthen embankment on his way home, he noticed a crack, about a finger's width, running along it. John Gunson the chief engineer turned out with one of the contractors to inspect the dam. They had to make the 8 miles (12.9km) from Sheffield in a horse-drawn gig, in deteriorating weather conditions, so it was 10pm before they got there. After an initial

Dale Dike Reservoir

3h00 — 5.5 MILES — 8.8 KM — LEVEL 1 2 3

MAP: OS Explorer OL1 Dark Peak

START/FINISH: by the cricket ground in Bradfield, off Fairhouse Lane on The Sands, grid ref: SK 262920

PATHS: minor roads, bridleways, forest paths, 10 stiles and gates

LANDSCAPE: woodland, reservoir and meadows

PUBLIC TOILETS: none on route

TOURIST INFORMATION: Upper Derwent Valley, tel 01433 650953

THE PUB: The Plough, Low Bradfield, at the end of the walk before returning to the start

Getting to the start

From the A57 Sheffield to Manchester road, take the minor road 3 miles (4.8km) east of Ladybower Reservoir, signed for Strines Inn. Go first right, second left, then first left to Bradfield. The car park is at the north west end of the village, along The Sands off Fairhouse Lane.

Researched and written by: Neil Coates, Moira McCrossan, Hugh Taylor

inspection, Gunson concluded that it was nothing to worry about. However as a precaution he decided to lower the water level. He re-inspected the crack at 11.30pm and just had time to scramble up the side before a large section of the dam collapsed, unleashing a solid wall of water down into the valley below towards Sheffield.

The torrent destroyed everything in its path and though the waters started to subside within half an hour, their force swept aside 415 houses, 106 factories and shops, 20 bridges and countless cottage and market gardens for 8 miles (12.9km).

At the inquest the jury concluded that there had been insufficient engineering skill devoted to a work of such size and called for legislation to ensure 'frequent, sufficient and regular' inspections of dams. The Dale Dike Dam was rebuilt in 1875 but it was not brought into full use until 1887, a very dry year.

the walk

1 From the car park return to **Fairhouse Lane** and turn right towards **Strines**. Ignore the first turn right, but keep right at the next fork towards **Midhopestones**. The lane rises, passing **Haychatter House** and bends round above **Upper Thornseat**. When the road turns sharply right, at the entrance to **Thompson House**, turn left on to the farm road, marked as a bridleway.

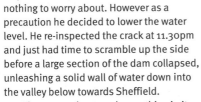

what to look for

A memorial was erected at the dam in 1991 to commemorate those who lost their lives in the flood. It's a simple memorial stone surrounded by a small garden. Next to it there's a white stone bearing the letters CLOB. This is one of four stones that mark the Centre Line of the Old Bank and are the only trace today of where the earthen embankment of the previous dam stood.

2 From here go through a gate in front of you and on to **Hall Lane**, a public bridleway. Follow this along the edge of a wood then through another gate and continue right on the farm road. Another gate at the end of this road leads to the entrance to **Hallfield**.

3 The right of way goes through the grounds of Hallfield but an alternative permissive path leads left over a stile, round the perimeter of the house and across another stile to re-join the bridleway at the back of the house. Follow the bridleway through two gates and then past **Stubbin Farm**.

4 The next gate leads to **Brogging Farm** and the dam at the head of Strines Reservoir. Look out for a sign near the end of the farmhouse and turn left. Go slightly downhill, over a stile, follow the path, then cross a stile and go through a wood.

5 Cross the stream by a footbridge, keep right, ignoring a second footbridge to reach a low waymark post. Fork left along the permissive path, then follow the path along the bank of **Dale Dike Reservoir** to the dam head. From here continue through the woods, down several sets of steps and continue on the path looking out for the memorial to those who were killed as a result of the dam breaching in 1864.

6 Follow the path until it reaches the road. Cross the stile, turn right on to the road and proceed to the Y-Junction. Turn sharp right, cross the bridge then look for a public footpath sign to Low Bradfield, just before the entrance to **Doe House** drive. Cross the stile on the left and follow the path. The path crosses two stiles then terminates at a T-junction with **Mill Lee Road** opposite the **Plough Inn**. Turn left and follow this road downhill, through the village and back to the car park.

The Plough

Bradfield

SOUTH YORKSHIRE

about the pub

The Plough
New Road, Low Bradfield
near Sheffield, S6 6HW
Tel 0114 2851 280

DIRECTIONS: from the car park turn left into Fairhouse Lane, continue to Mill Lee Road then go left into New Road

PARKING: 40

OPEN: daily, all day Saturday (in summer) and Sunday

FOOD: daily

BREWERY/COMPANY: free house

REAL ALE: Caledonian Deuchars IPA, guest beer

DOGS: allowed in taproom only

Expect a genuine warm welcome at this former farmhouse on the edge of the village. From the roadside the 200-year-old exterior may look a little time-worn but from the rear the prospect is more pleasing, with plenty of colourful hanging baskets, flower tubs, a climbing rose or two, and a shady beer garden with views to the rising moors and the wooded valley of Dale Dike. The main dining room is housed in a converted barn, with enormous windows, a huge stone fireplace and the pub piano. Local watercolours adorn the walls in the adjacent open-plan bar, while a pool table and dart board can be found in the basic taproom bar where locals congregate to quaff pints of Deuchars IPA. A classic village local.

Food

At lunch tuck into home-made soup, Stilton and vegetable crumble, daily curries and deep-filled pies, a mixed grill, or jacket potatoes with various fillings. The extensive evening menu takes in black pudding melt, braised lamb shank, fish and chips and a 'sizzling skillet' with sweet and sour prawns. There are traditional roast lunches on Sunday.

Family facilities

Children are welcome in the main bar where they have their own standard menu. There is a play area in the garden.

Alternative refreshment stops

Buy picnic supplies from the shop near the village green

☛ Where to go from here

Sheffield's fascinating industrial heritage is celebrated in a number of hands-on working museums such as those at Kelham Island and Abbeydale Industrial Hamlet (www.simt.co.uk).

Chatsworth Park and Gardens

Chatsworth

DERBYSHIRE

A stroll along the River Derwent past gardens and through parkland created by 18th-century landscape guru Lancelot 'Capability' Brown.

Chatsworth House

Sitting on the banks of the River Derwent, surrounded by lush green parkland, moors and a backdrop of wooded hillsides, Chatsworth is one of the most elegant and popular of England's stately homes. First opened to the public in 1844 it continues to attract large numbers of visitors.

Work first started on the house in 1549 when Sir William Cavendish acquired the land and set about building a mansion. He died before it was completed and it was finished by his widow, Bess of Hardwick, who by the simple expedient of marrying four times, each time to a more powerful and rich man, succeeded in becoming the richest woman in England after the Queen. She also built the magnificent Elizabethan house of Hardwick Hall, some 15 miles (24km) to the east, which is now in the care of the National Trust. Bess left Chatsworth to her son Henry Cavendish, who sold it to his brother William, the 1st Earl of Devonshire. It has now been home to fourteen generations of the Cavendish family and is the seat of the current Duke and Duchess of Devonshire.

Initially a three-storey Elizabethan mansion, the house has been altered and added to over the centuries. The 4th Earl, who was later made 1st Duke of Devonshire for his support of William III in the 'Glorious Revolution' of 1688, practically rebuilt it.

Towards the end of the 18th century the 4th Duke had the magnificent baroque stables built and engaged the services of landscape gardener Lancelot 'Capability' Brown. Brown dramatically altered the 100-acre (40ha) garden that the 1st Duke had created in the 1690s and laid out the 1,000-acre (450ha) park surrounding the house. Magnificent as Chatsworth House is, it is the gardens and parkland that draw visitors back again and again. There are rare trees, sculptures, fountains and gardens, as well as a maze, estate farm and adventure playground for children.

The Emperor Fountain in the long canal pond, built in 1844 by Chatsworth's head gardener Joseph Paxton, is the highest gravity fed fountain in the world. Paxton designed a lake in the hills above the garden to store water for the fountain. He was knighted by Queen Victoria and is buried in the churchyard at Edensor.

Edensor was mentioned in the Domesday Book but the 4th Duke had the original village demolished because some of the houses interfered with his view. He rebuilt it as a model village, using local stone, with each building in a different architectural style. It's still home to estate workers and pensioners.

the walk

1 From **Edensor** village cross the B6012 and take the footpath to the right-hand side of the large tree. Walk across the parkland to join the main drive to **Chatsworth House** near a bridge. Cross over the road and trace a wood-rail fence to the riverbank, then walk downstream with the river on your left.

Chatsworth House sits in the wooded valley of the Derwent River which flows through the estate

3h00 **5.5 MILES** **8.8 KM** **LEVEL 1**

MAP: OS Explorer OL24 White Peak
START/FINISH: Edensor village, grid ref
SK 251699
PATHS: good paths and forest trails
LANDSCAPE: parkland, woodland
and moorland
PUBLIC TOILETS: at Chatsworth
TOURIST INFORMATION: Bakewell,
tel 01629 813227
THE PUB: The Devonshire Arms, The Square,
Beeley, see Directions to the pub, page 155

Getting to the start

Edensor village and Chatsworth are located
on the B6012 east of the A6 Buxton to
Matlock road. The village car park is just
off the B6012.

Researched and written by:
Neil Coates, Moira McCrossan, Hugh Taylor

*Taking a break while walking through
the White Peaks*

2 Follow the **River Derwent** past a couple
of weirs and the remains of an
imposing old mill to the next bridge that
carries the B6012 over the river. To the right
of the bridge a metal kissing gate allows
access to the road. Cross the bridge.

3 Ignore the left turn into the drive past a
gatehouse to the estate, but take the
next immediate left along the other side of
the gatehouse and continue uphill, past a
renovated barn on the right and then a
striking farmhouse. Just past the last barn in
the complex, and as the road roughens, look
on the left for a stile and a worn fingerpost
for Robin Hood and Hunting Tower.

4 Cross the field half right, go over the
next stile and go diagonally left, uphill
following the waymarkers on a well-defined
path. When this meets a wider track at the
hillcrest go left, cross the wall into the
estate via a high stile and walk ahead
150yds (138m), bending right to a cross-
tracks. Here, go ahead with the sign for
Robin Hood along a wide hard-core track.

5 Remain with this past the **Swiss Lake** on
your right and then loop around the top
of **Emperor Lake** on your left. Some 300yds

what to look for

Visit Edensor church rebuilt in 1869, which contains the remnants of its 14th-century predecessor, including the monuments to William and Henry Cavendish, the sons of Bess of Hardwick. Also buried within the church is Lord Frederick Cavendish. He was Irish Secretary in Gladstone's government when he was hacked to death in Phoenix Park in Dublin in 1882, along with his Under-Secretary Thomas Burke, by a group of extreme Irish nationalists called the Invincibles.

6 Walk immediately left of the **Tower** and down some rough steps below small canons to turn left along a tarred lane, shortly ignoring the turn off to the right. The lane heads gently downhill, past what appears to be the remains of an old viaduct with water cascading from the end, then doubles back, still going downhill, eventually reaching the car park at **Chatsworth House** a short stride beyond the entrance to the farmyard.

(274m) beyond here the track is crossed by a narrow footpath; the **Hunting Tower** is visible left along this.

7 Walk down through the car park to join the lane leading ahead out of the parkland. Cross the ornate bridge and fork right along the path that returns you to **Edensor**.

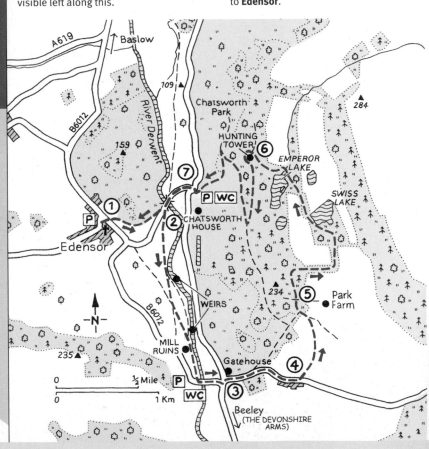

The Devonshire Arms

Built of honey-coloured stone, this handsome old inn stands tucked away in a picture-postcard estate village on the edge of Chatsworth Park. Originally three separate cottages, it was converted into a popular coaching inn in 1747. Charles Dickens was a frequent visitor, and it is rumoured that King Edward VII met here with his mistress, Alice Keppel. Today, you'll be greeted by oak beams, stone flagged floors, stripped stone walls, antique settles, farmhouse tables, and roaring winter log fires. A civilised atmosphere pervades the comfortable lounge bar and dining areas; there's a separate, more rustic taproom where walkers with muddy boots are welcome. Excellent Black Sheep and Theakston ales are on tap, alongside a good list of wines, and numerous malt whiskies.

Food

Traditional home-cooked bar food is available all day and ranges from freshly made soups with crusty bread, four-cheese ploughman's lunches and Cumberland sausage, to beef and horseradish pudding, lamb hotpot and smoked haddock rarebit.

about the pub

The Devonshire Arms
The Square, Beeley
Bakewell, Derbyshire DE4 2NR
Tel 01629 733259

DIRECTIONS: from Edensor head south on the B6012 for 3 miles (4.8km). The pub is in the centre of Beeley	
PARKING: 50	
OPEN: daily, all day	
FOOD: daily, all day	
BREWERY/COMPANY: free house	
REAL ALE: Black Sheep Bitter and Special, Theakston Old Peculier, guest beers	
DOGS: not allowed inside	

A Victorian breakfast is served on Sundays (10am until noon), and there's also a special fish night on Fridays.

Family facilities

Children are welcome throughout the pub and there's a children's menu for youngsters to choose from. On fine days you can enjoy delightful village views from the front patio seating.

Alternative refreshment stops

Chatsworth's dining options are set out around the courtyard. The Carriage House, enclosed by glass walling, offers an excellent choice of meals in a self-service, fully licensed restaurant. Light refreshments are available in the nearby Covered Ride and Jean Pierre's Bar.

☛ Where to go from here

Britain's favourite stately home, Chatsworth, also has an estate farm and woodland adventure playground. (www.chatsworth.org). Haddon Hall is in the area, near Bakewell (www.haddonhall.co.uk).

Cromford and the Black Rocks

Walk through the Industrial Revolution in a valley where history was made.

Cromford

For centuries Cromford was no more than a sleepy backwater. Lead mining brought the village brief prosperity, but by the 18th century even that was in decline. Everything changed in 1771 when Sir Richard Arkwright built the world's first watered-powered cotton-spinning mill here. Within 20 years he had built two more, and had constructed a whole new town around them. Cromford was awake to the Industrial Revolution and would be connected to the rest of Britain by a network of roads, railways and canals.

As you walk through the courtyard of the Arkwright Mill, now being restored by the Arkwright Society, you are transported back to the 18th century, to the times when mother, father and children all worked at the mills. Most of the town lies on the other side of the A6, including the mill pond built by Arkwright to impound the waters of Bonsall Brook, and the restored mill workers' cottages of North Street.

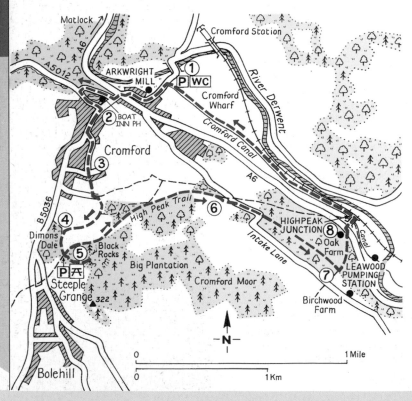

The Black Rocks overlook the town from the south. The walk makes a beeline for them through little ginnels, past some almshouses and through pine woods. There's a good path all the way to the top. Here you can look across the Derwent Valley to the beacon on top of Crich Stand and down the Derwent Gorge to Matlock.

The route then takes you on to the High Peak Trail, which uses the former trackbed of the Cromford and High Peak Railway. Engineered by Josias Jessop, and built in the 1830s the railway was built as an extension of the canal system and, as such, the stations were called wharfs. In the early years horses pulled the wagons on the level stretches, while steam-winding engines worked the inclines. By the mid-1800s steam engines worked the whole line, which connected with the newly extended Midland Railway. The railway was closed by Dr Beeching in 1967.

After leaving the High Peak Trail forest paths descend into the valley at High Peak Junction, where the old railway met the Cromford Canal. The canal was built in 1793, a year after Arkwright's death, to link up with the Erewash, thus completing a navigable waterway to the River Trent at Trent Lock. Today, there's a fascinating information centre here to visit before returning along the towpath to Cromford.

3h00 — **5 MILES** — **8 KM** — **LEVEL 1**23

WALK

Cromford

DERBYSHIRE

MAP: OS Explorer OL24 White Peak
START/FINISH: Cromford Wharf pay car park, grid ref SK 300571
PATHS: well-graded – canal tow paths, lanes, forest paths and a railway trackbed, about 20 stiles and gates
LANDSCAPE: town streets and wooded hillsides
PUBLIC TOILETS: at car park
TOURIST INFORMATION: Matlock Bath, tel 01629 55082
THE PUB: The Boat Inn, Cromford, see Point **1** on route

❶ The long, steady climb from Cromford to Black Rocks is best suited to older children. There are steep, unprotected drops at Black Rocks

Getting to the start

Cromford is on the A6 about 3 miles (4.8km) south of Matlock. Parking in Market Place is restricted, so use the pay car park at Cromford Wharf, well signed and to the east of the main traffic lights on the A6 along Mill Road just below Arkwright's Mill.

Researched and written by:
Neil Coates, Moira McCrossan, Hugh Taylor

the walk

1 Turn left out of the car park on to **Mill Road**. Cross the A6 to **Market Place**. Turn right down the **Scarthin**, pass the **Boat Inn** and the **millpond** then double back left along **Water Lane** to **Cromford Hill**.

Cromford Canal

2 Turn right, past the shops and **Bell Inn,** then turn left up **Bedehouse Lane,** which turns into a narrow tarmac ginnel after rounding some almshouses (otherwise known as bedehouses).

3 At the top of the lane by a street of 1970s housing, a signpost for **Black Rocks** points uphill. The footpath continues its climb southwards to meet a lane. Turn left along the winding lane, which soon divides. Take the right fork, a limestone track leading to a stone-built house with woods behind. On reaching the house, turn right through a gate, and follow the top field edge.

4 Climb some steps up a wall and walk ahead across the derelict land to find a wide path that climbs left through the woods of **Dimons Dale** up to the **Black Rocks car park** and picnic site. The track you've reached is on the former trackbed of the Cromford and High Peak Railway. Immediately opposite is the there-and-back waymarked detour leading to the rocks.

5 Returning to the car park, turn right along the **High Peak Trail** towards High Peak Junction, which traverses the hillside high above Cromford.

what to look for

Besides the Arkwright Mill, which is a 'must see' venue, take some time to visit the exhibits in old railway workshops at High Peak Junction and the Leawood Pumping Station, which pumped water from the River Derwent to the Cromford Canal. The restored Leawood works has a working Cornish-type beam engine.

6 After about 0.75 mile (1.2km) you'll reach the top of **Sheep Pasture Incline.** Descend this to a fingerpost near the bottom, pointing the path right for **Alderwasley** and **the Midshires Way.** Gradually climb this wide, sandy forest track (Intake Lane) to a sharp right-hand bend. Here, go straight on, following a path heading south east within the top edge of some woodland. (**Note:** neither the path nor the wood is shown on the current Ordnance Survey Explorer OL map of the White Peak.)

7 This path passes behind a **chalet** and **caravan park** and then is joined by a path coming in sharply from the left. Soon after this there's a gateway (right) with a corrugated iron barn visible at the field top. At this waymarked gateway you should turn left down a grooved path descending steeply through the trees. At the bottom of the woods the path swings left across fields, coming out to the A6 road by **Oak Farm.**

8 Cross the road and follow the little ginnel opposite, over the **Matlock railway** and the **Cromford Canal.** Go past the **High Peak Junction Information Centre,** then turn left along the canal tow path. Follow this back to the car park at **Cromford Wharf.**

The restored Arkwright Mill dates from 1771 and was powered by a water mill on the River Derwent

The Boat Inn

about the pub
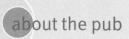

The Boat Inn
Off Market Place, Scarthin
Cromford, Derbyshire DE4 3QF
Tel 01629 823282
www.theboatatcromford.co.uk

DIRECTIONS: see Point 1 in the route directions	
PARKING: 10	
OPEN: daily, all day Saturday and Sunday	
FOOD: no food Sunday or Monday evening	
BREWERY/COMPANY: free house	
REAL ALE: Marston's Pedigree, Springhead Bitter, two guest beers	
DOGS: welcome in the bar	

Dated 1772 and tucked away off the Market Square in Cromford, this popular free house was originally built to serve the staff at Arkwright's Mill. The millworkers used to slake their thirst here while the managers and directors used the neighbouring Greyhound Hotel. Today, the Boat is a cracking locals' pub and allegedly haunted by three ghosts – a little girl, the 'traditional' grey lady and a Roman centurion. Bare stone walls, low-beamed ceilings, log fires and nautical bric-a-brac create a cosy, relaxed atmosphere, with the added attractions of Springhead beers on tap and good value food drawing loyal regulars and weary walkers.

Food
Popular light lunchtime bites include sandwiches, filled baguettes and cheese and vegetable quiche with salad. More substantial dishes range from steak, mushroom and ale pie to daily specials like roast lamb shank in minted red wine gravy, and Yorkshire pudding with sausages in onion and red wine sauce.

Family facilities
On fine days retreat with the children to the sun-trap tiered garden and patio behind the pub. Children are also made welcome inside and they have a standard menu to choose from.

Alternative refreshment stops
Arkwright's Mill has a small café.

☛ Where to go from here
If you have time, visit Wirksworth, a former lead mining town on the hillsides above Cromford. Take a look at the National Stone Centre on Portway Lane. Here you can have a go at gem panning and join guided walks. The Wirksworth Heritage Centre, which is housed in a former silk and velvet mill at Crown Yard, gives a fascinating insight into the town's history.

Middleton Top and the High Peak Trail

CYCLE

Fascinating industrial heritage and huge views on this moderate ride along an old railway designed and engineered as a canal.

High Peak Trail

The High Peak Trail is an engineering marvel. It follows the trackbed of the Cromford and High Peak Railway, built between 1825 and 1830, and was one of the world's first railways. Curiously, it was designed as a canal to link the Cromford Canal at Cromford, in the Derwent Valley, with the Upper Peak Forest tramroad and canal network in the Goyt Valley, south east of Manchester. The promoters eventually realised that water supply would be an insurmountable problem, so the route was redrafted as a railway, with the planned flights of locks replaced by steep inclines (the stations, however, retained their watery origins and were known as 'Wharfs'). One such incline tops-out at Middleton Top. Here, the engine house that provided the steam power to drive the ropes that winched the wagons up these slopes is still operational, and regular steamings are held each year. The nearby Hopton Incline was, at 1:14, the steepest gradient to be used by standard steam locomotives during the mid-20th century.

the ride

1 Take time to explore **Middleton Top** before setting out along the long straight westwards. The first feature of interest is the short **Hopton Tunnel**, a covered access to one of the many local quarries that dapple these limestone slopes around Middleton Moor. The track then passes above one of the large surviving works that still makes use of the abundant limestone – cement is a major product here.

2 After this easy start you'll soon reach the foot of the **Hopton Incline**. This is the last of the inclines used to raise the railway up from the Derwent Valley; this particular one is a steep 1:14; challenging, but an easier gradient than some of the others. Ride it or walk it, but once at the top you can take in the first of the views that characterise the High Peak Trail. At the incline top is another old incline house, while south is a ruinous windmill tower on Carsington Pasture. Secreted beyond these windy upland pastures is the valley of the Henmore Brook, now flooded as **Carsington Water**.

3 One advantage of these inclines is a very easy gradient. Once past the incline house there are several long straights and gentle curves and only a few shallow cuttings to spoil the views. Another works is passed at the foot of the stepped hillside of **Harboro Rocks**; this is renowned locally for rock climbing. A long curve

Cyclists passing an old quarry near Minninglow

exposes distant views to the north across the Peak District before the industrial hamlet of **Longcliffe** is reached. Surviving here are an engine shed and, more unusually, a watering ramp. Tankers of water would be stationed here to allow the locomotives to take on water in an area otherwise largely devoid of this vital resource. This is one opportunity to turn around – the return distance from the start is 7 miles (11.3km).

4 Continuing north west soon brings you to an incredible **viewpoint** across the north Midlands – more than 40 miles (64.3km) on a clear day. Near to hand are the unusual, craggy wooded hilltops above **Brassington; Rainster Rocks** and **Black Rocks** were home to Iron-Age families. The character of the route begins to change. Long straights on barely-raised banks of ballast or shallow cuttings give way to more extensive engineering works. A length of wood fencing to each side of the track shields you from the winds as you cross the first of a series of embankments that make the Cromford and High Peak line one of the wonders of the early railway age.

5 A little further along, a more substantial embankment is crossed. This does not have any fencing so ensure that inexperienced children are well supervised. Beyond the embankment is the rusty remnant of an old quarry crane. The most spectacular embankment comes into view as you approach **Minninglow**.

6 The picnic area beyond here is an ideal place to terminate your outward journey before returning to Middleton Top.

| 4h00 | 13 MILES | 21 KM | LEVEL 2 |

SHORTER ALTERNATIVE ROUTE

| 2h30 | 7 MILES | 11.3 KM | LEVEL 1 |

MAP: OS Explorer OL24 White Peak

START/FINISH: Middleton Top car park and visitor centre, grid ref SK275552

TRAILS/TRACKS: Old railway trackbed throughout; compacted stone or cinder surfaces

LANDSCAPE: edge of the White Peak Plateau, with dramatic views across the north Midlands

PUBLIC TOILETS: Middleton Top

TOURIST INFORMATION: Matlock Bath, tel 01629 55082

CYCLE HIRE: Middleton Top, tel 01629 823204

THE PUB: The Rising Sun, Middleton, see Directions to the pub, page 163

❗ Generally easy riding but note the 1:14 Hopton Incline and the unfenced embankment at Point 5

Getting to the start

Middleton Top car park on the High Peak Trail, just south west of Cromford, is signposted off the B5035 Ashbourne to Cromford road.

Why do this cycle ride?

There is some fascinating industrial heritage hereabouts, much of which can seen along the High Peak Trail. This route can be as long or short as you choose; the old railway climbs up inclines, strides across massive embankments and reveals superb views deep into the Midlands. Whether you're intent on an hour's ride or an afternoon's outing, this is the ideal route for a family group.

Researched and written by: Neil Coates

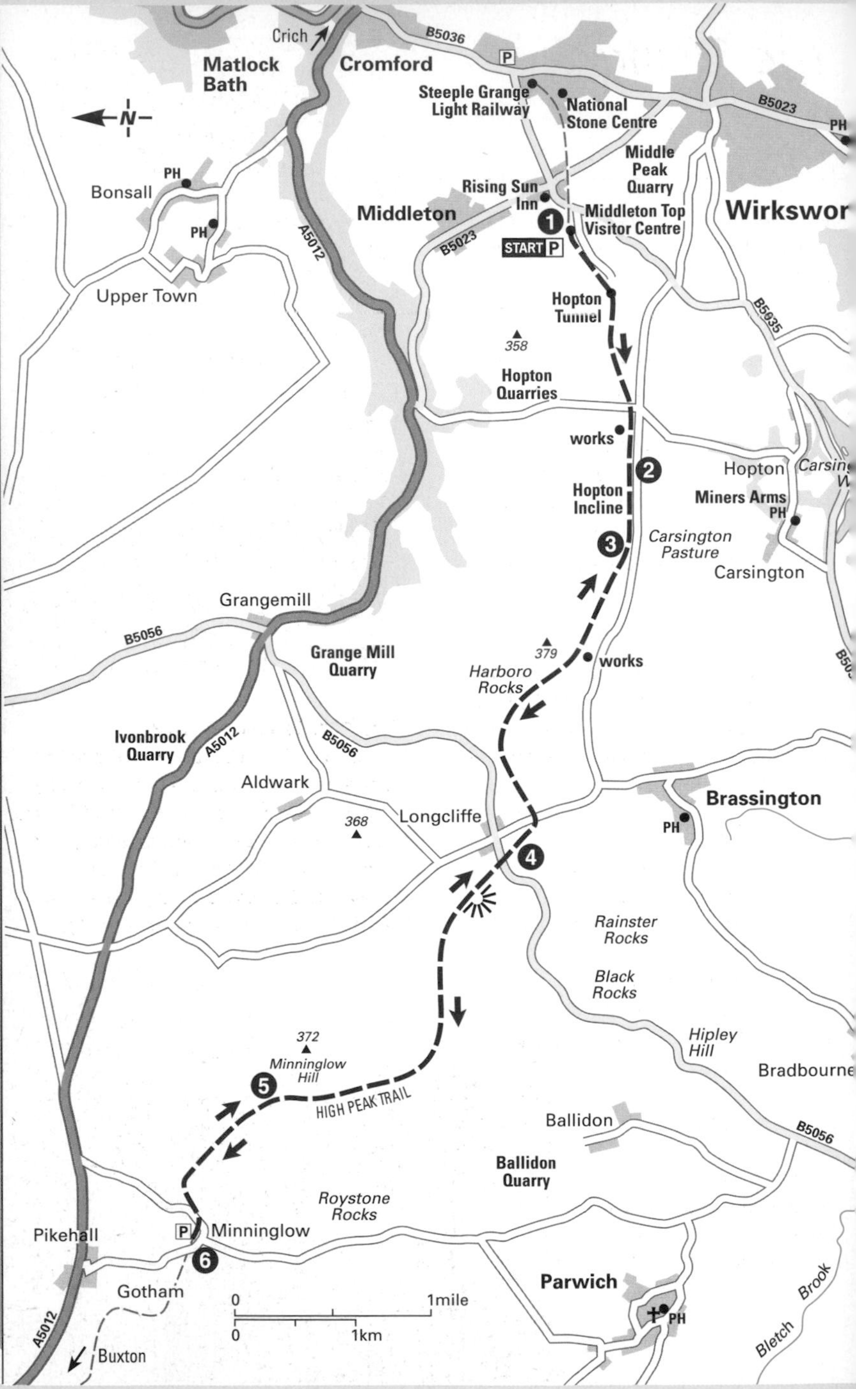

Crich

Matlock Bath

Cromford

B5036

P

B5023

PH

Steeple Grange Light Railway

National Stone Centre

Middle Peak Quarry

PH

Bonsall

PH

Rising Sun Inn

Middleton

B5023

1

START P

Middleton Top Visitor Centre

Wirkswor

Upper Town

Hopton Tunnel

B5035

▲ 358

Hopton Quarries

works

Hopton

Carsin W

2

Miners Arms

PH

Hopton Incline

Carsington Pasture

3

Carsington

Grangemill

B5056

Grange Mill Quarry

▲ 379

Harboro Rocks

works

Ivonbrook Quarry

A5012

B5056

Aldwark

Longcliffe

Brassington

PH

▲ 368

4

Rainster Rocks

Black Rocks

Hipley Hill

▲ 372

Minninglow Hill

5

HIGH PEAK TRAIL

Bradbourne

Ballidon

B5056

Pikehall

P Minninglow

6

Roystone Rocks

Ballidon Quarry

Gotham

0 ——— 1mile

0 ——— 1km

Parwich

† PH

Bletch Brook

Buxton

A5012

← —N—

The Rising Sun

Located on the edge of this old industrial village, the Rising Sun is an unpretentious and thriving community pub that offers a genuine welcome to all. Following your exertions on the High Peak Trails, it is a friendly place to relax in, with a lively bar and taproom plus a couple of quieter side rooms for families. The beer is good and the food home cooked. It is simply furnished throughout, with benches and traditional pub tables and chairs on quarry tiled or boarded floors, and one room features a changing gallery of paintings by a local artist.

Food

Expect traditional pub food in the form of lasagne, Brie crumble, mixed grill, plaice stuffed with prawns and mushroom sauce and fish pie. There's also a good range of sandwiches and filled potatoes.

Family facilities

Families are welcome to sit and eat in the two side rooms off the bar. There's a bargain standard children's menu and smaller portions are available. The small side garden is ideal for summer eating and drinking, or a game of boules.

Alternative refreshment stops

There is a snack bar at Middleton Top. The Miner's Arms in Brassington is about 1 mile (1.6km) off the route.

about the pub

The Rising Sun
Rise End
Middleton-by-Wirksworth
Derbyshire DE4 4LS
Tel 01629 822420

DIRECTIONS: load up your bikes from the Middleton Top car park and return to the main road and turn left. The Rising Sun is on the left soon after passing beneath the railway bridge

PARKING: 30

OPEN: daily, all day

FOOD: daily

BREWERY/COMPANY: Punch Taverns

REAL ALE: Tetley, Marston's Pedigree, guest beer

ROOMS: 3 bedrooms

☛ Where to go from here

The National Stone Centre near Middleton is full of geological and industrial wonders explaining the structure of the Peak District, and you can take part in gem panning and fossil-rubbing. The National Tramway Museum at Crich offers vintage tram travel in period streets (www.tramway.co.uk).

The Heights of Abraham

A steady climb raises you above the hurley burley of Matlock Bath to a more familiar Peakland landscape.

Matlock Bath and the Derwent Valley
Between Matlock and Cromford the River Derwent forges its way through a spectacular, thickly wooded limestone gorge. At Matlock Bath it jostles for space with the bustling A6 highway, the railway to Derby and a string of three-storey houses, shops and amusement parlours, built by

the Victorians, who flocked here to take in the healing spa waters. On the hillside to the east lies the gaunt castle of Riber, while Alpine-type cable cars glide up the Heights of Abraham, above cliff tops to the west. The original Heights of Abraham rise above Quebec and the St Lawrence River in Canada. There, in 1759, British troops under General Wolfe fought a victorious battle with the French under General Montcalm.

Matlock Bath is Derbyshire's mini-Blackpool, yet there are peaceful corners, and this fine walk seeks them out. It climbs through the woods and out on to the hillside

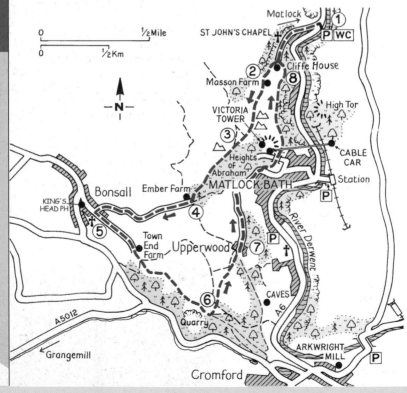

2h30	4.5 MILES	7 KM	LEVEL 2

MAP: OS Explorer OL24 White Peak

START/FINISH: Matlock: pay car park at Artists Corner, grid ref SK 297595

PATHS: narrow woodland paths, field paths and unsurfaced lanes, 10 stiles and gates

LANDSCAPE: fields and wooded hillsides

PUBLIC TOILETS: at car park

TOURIST INFORMATION: Matlock Bath, tel 01629 55082

THE PUB: King's Head, Bonsall, see Point **4** on route

🚸 This walk has a long, and in some places, steep opening section before levelling out beside the Heights of Abraham leisure park

Getting to the start

Matlock is on the A6 between Buxton and Matlock. The car park at Artists Corner is well signed.

Researched and written by:
Neil Coates, John Gillham

Top: The River Derwent running through Matlock Bath
Page 166: Looking across the Heights of Abraham to Riber Castle

above the town. The Victoria Prospect Tower peeps over the trees. Built by unemployed miners a century ago it's now part of the Heights of Abraham complex. Above the complex, a little path leads you through woodland. In spring it's heavy with the scent of wild garlic and coloured by a carpet of bluebells. Out of the woods, an attractive hedge-lined unsurfaced lane weaves its way through high pastures, giving distant views of the White Peak plateau, Black Rocks and the cliffs of Crich Stand.

At the end of the lane is Bonsall, whose perpendicular church tower and spire has been beckoning you for some time. In the centre of this old lead mining village is a market square with a 17th-century cross. The lane out of Bonsall takes you to the edge of an area of old mine shafts and modern-day quarries. The route goes north, back into the woods of the Derwent Valley, passing the high hamlet of Upperwood, where fleeting views of Matlock and Matlock Bath appear through the trees.

Right: Cable cars heading up to the Heights of Abraham

the walk

1 Cross the A6, then take **St John's Road** up the wooded slopes opposite. It passes beneath **St John's Chapel** to reach the gates of **Cliffe House**. Take the path on the right signed **'To the Heights of Abraham'**. The path climbs steeply beside the estate wall through the woodland edge; scramble over a high, broken stone step stile and veer left to another stile into the rough fields above **Masson Farm**.

2 The footpath continues to an old gateway and waymark post, with **Victoria Prospect Tower** directly ahead. Turn right beyond the gateway, and rise to a stile at the top of the field. Beyond this the footpath threads through hawthorn thickets before passing a small gated entry (left) into the **Heights of Abraham** complex.

3 Ignore this and continue uphill for about 30yds (27m), then turn left over a stile (waymarked **Derwent Valley Walk**). After crossing a tarred access road, the narrow footpath re-enters woodland.

4 At the far side of the woods turn right along a farm lane, passing well below **Ember Farm**. This pleasant walled lane winds down pastured hillslopes into Bonsall village. To find the **King's Head** turn right at the lane; it's about 200yds (183m) along here. Then return to this spot.

what to look for

St John's Chapel, seen early in the walk, was designed and built in 1897 by Sir Guy Dauber for Mrs Harris, who lived at Rock House, a short way down the hill. It was meant to serve the parishioners who found it difficult to reach St Giles at Matlock, but it was also a place for those who preferred a High Church service.

5 Turn left past the school along a lane that becomes unsurfaced when you get beyond **Town End Farm**. This track climbs gently as a wide track around the fenced perimeter of the quarry to reach an old gateway across the narrowing track at the edge of woods; there's also a waymark arrow ahead and an old stone gatepost here.

6 Don't go ahead, but look left for a squeeze stile into pasture. Follow the path straight across to another stile into woods. Drop down to an old lane at a ruinous barn. Take the lower track, past a rusty gate, and walk through to the stub-end of a tarred lane.

7 This is the hamlet of **Upperwood**. Walk ahead across the turning area and around the left bend, remaining with this narrow tarred lane between cottages for nearly 0.5 mile (800m) to pass the lodge-house entrance to the **Heights of Abraham** showcave. Just around the next bend, leave the lane for a stepped path through the woods on the left, signposted **'Public Footpath to Matlock'**. Climb some steps to a high wooden footbridge over the **Heights of Abraham** approach road, and then continue on the woodland path. You'll pass under the Heights of Abraham cable cars (not easily seen) before eventually joining a track that has come in from the left.

8 This track joins **St John's Lane** and the outward route at **Cliffe House**. Retrace your steps back to the start.

King's Head

Tiny, diamond-leaded windows, thick, weathered stone mullions and the mellowed stone structure to the cosy and homely King's Head indicate the pub's great age. Local word says that it was opened on the day King Charles I was executed in January 1649, although a more reliable date is the 1677 included in the structure. Outside, it is awash with colourful hanging baskets and flower tubs; inside are the Yeoman's Bar and the King's Lounge, both full of atmosphere. Expect darkwood panelling, glowing wood-burning stoves in winter, old benches and pews, a wealth of porcelain and china, and scrubbed tables topped with candles and fresh flowers. Don't forget tip-top ales from Bateman's and a good blackboard menu. It stands in the tiny market square next to the remarkable stepped Market Cross.

Food

Look to the chalkboard for steak and kidney pudding, parsnip and sweet potato bake, Caribbean lamb, Barnsley lamb chop, and a choice of fresh fish, perhaps including trout with prawn and garlic sauce. At lunchtime expect sandwiches and lighter meals.

Family facilities

Children will enjoy the pub's characterful interior – they are welcome throughout. They can choose from their own menu and eat al fresco in the sheltered courtyard on sunny days.

Alternative refreshment stops

The Barley Mow in the Dale just off the Via Gellia offers real ale and has a reputation for excellent food.

☞ Where to go from here

The Peak District Mining Museum at Matlock Bath Pavilion on the A6 alongside the River Derwent has reconstructed mines to explore and crawl through (www.peakmines.co.uk).

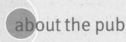

about the pub

King's Head
62 Yeoman Street, Bonsall
Derbyshire DE4 2AA
Tel 01629 822703

DIRECTIONS: in Bonsall village, near Point **5** on the route	
PARKING: 10	
OPEN: closed Monday lunch	
FOOD: daily	
BREWERY/COMPANY: Bateman's	
REAL ALE: Bateman's XB, Dark Mild, seasonal beers	
DOGS: welcome throughout	

Crich and the Cromford Canal

WALK

On Crich Chase through TV-land to the monument of Crich Stand.

Crich

A short section of busy main road at the start is soon forgotten on this varied walk. As soon as you've crossed the old canal via Chase Bridge you're in a different world. An ivy clad wall blocks sight and sound of the road and the railway while the canal, tangled with irises and pondweed, ambles by slowly through the trees. Watch out for the bright yellow and black spotted longhorn beetle feeding on the meadowsweet and the holly blue butterflies, which flutter around the bridge in springtime.

On this journey you save the greater part of the canal walking to the end, in order to climb through the woodland of Crich Chase, once part of a hunting forest owned by the 13th-century Norman baron, Hubert FitzRalph. After climbing high fields and along a gritstone edge, known as the Tors, you come upon Crich (pronounced so the 'i' rhymes with eye) which was *Peak Practice*'s Cardale until the series moved to Longnor in 2001. Past the market cross and across more fields you come to the National Tramway Museum, which is well worth a visit.

The walk continues to its high point on Crich Stand, a limestone crag isolated by an area of gritstone. Capping the Stand is a 60ft (19m) beacon tower, rebuilt in 1921 to commemorate the Sherwood Foresters killed in the two World Wars and more recent conflicts. On a clear day you can pick out Lincoln and its cathedral. Often you'll see kestrels hovering around the cliff edge, searching for their prey.

The Cromford Canal

The path descends through more woodland, beneath the gritstone cliffs of the old Dukes Quarry and down to the canal at Whatstandwell. The canal has silted up, and is a haven for wildlife. It's well known for its varieties of hoverfly, its azure damselflies and brown chinamark moths. Yellow irises and flowering rush, which has pink flowers, can be seen on the water's edge, while broad-leaved pondweed clogs the middle of the canal which doesn't seem to impede the moorhens or mallards.

the walk

1 Turn left from the pub car park along the busy A6. Cross safely away from the junction and shortly turn right along **Chase Road**, which cuts under the railway bridge and climbs to the **Cromford Canal**. Follow the tow path northwards (water on your right) to the next bridge.

2 Go over the bridge before following a footpath left, climbing into the woodland of **Crich Chase**. Keep ahead on the main path at a cross-paths. In the upper reaches of the wood the occasionally waymarked path passes through several glades; it then follows a wood-rail fence on the right at the top edge of the wood. Turn right over a stile and climb across two fields to reach **Chadwick Nick Lane**.

3 Turn right up the road. After 300yds (274m), just over the brow, a path on the left begins with some steps and a stile, and continues the easy climb northwards across numerous fields with stiles and gates – and by the rock outcrops of **The Tors**.

4 The path becomes an enclosed ginnel, which emerges on **Sandy Lane**. Follow this to the **Market Square**, where you turn left, then right at a **Bulling Lane sign** along **Coasthill**. Keeping left at a junction with **Jeffries Lane**, **Coasthill** leads to an unsurfaced lane. Where the lane ends, follow a path in the same direction across fields to join another lane by some houses. Follow this to **Carr Lane** and then turn right, passing the entrance to the **National Tramway Museum**.

5 Continue along the road to a sharp right-hand bend. Here, turn left along **Plaistow Green Road**; then fork left up the approach road to **Crich Stand**, topped by the **Sherwood Foresters Monument**. There's a small fee if you want to go up to the viewing platform on the monument, but otherwise continue along the public right of way on the right. The footpath, signed to Wakebridge and Plaistow, veers half right through shrubs and bramble, before circumnavigating Cliff Quarry on your left.

3h30 · **7.5 MILES** · **12.1 KM** · **LEVEL 2**

WALK

MAP: OS Explorer OL24 White Peak
START/FINISH: park at the Hurt Arms, Ambergate (please check with landord beforehand), grid ref SK 348516
PATHS: woodland and field paths and canal tow path, 16 stiles and gates
LANDSCAPE: woods and pastured hills
PUBLIC TOILETS: none on route
TOURIST INFORMATION: Matlock Bath, tel 01629 55082
THE PUB: Hurt Arms, Ambergate, see Point **1** on route

Getting to the start
Ambergate is on the A6 between Matlock and Belper. The Hurt Arms is at the junction with the A610 at the north end of the village.

Researched and written by:
Neil Coates, John Gillham

Crich DERBYSHIRE

The Transport Museum at Crich

what to look for

St Mary's Church was consecrated in 1135. It has a perpendicular spired west tower with a Norman north arcade and a 14th-century chancel. Inside there is a circular Norman font, which is unusually large, and many tombs, including the one of Sir William de Wakebridge, whose family was wiped out by the Plague.

6 The path crosses the museum's tram track near its terminus, before winding down the hillside through scrub woodland. It joins a wide track descending past **Wakebridge** and **Cliff Farms** before coming to a road.

7 Turn right along the road for a few paces, then turn left on a footpath signposted **'To the Cromford Canal'**. This descends south across a long field before swinging right to enter a wood. A well-defined path passes beneath quarried rockfaces, and crosses a minor road before reaching the **canal** at **Whatstandwell**.

8 Cross the footbridge and turn left to gain the tow path, following this (water to your left) a most delightful 2 miles (3.2km) through the shade of tree boughs. At **Chase Bridge** is a waymark post signed for **Ambergate Station**. From here you retrace the outward route back to the pub.

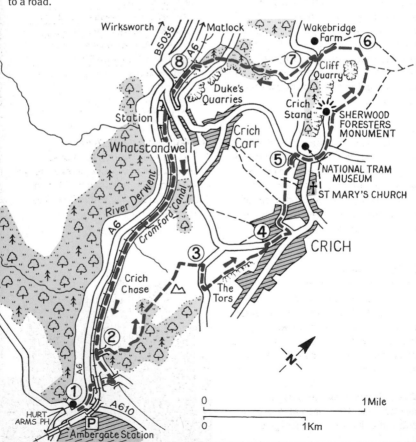

Hurt Arms

This imposing old country house was built of local stone in 1874 for a member of the local landowning family and stands next to the village cricket pitch, just a stone's throw from the River Derwent. Despite fronting the main A6, its grounds stretch back beneath tall limes, allowing extensive patios and gardens to be enjoyed. Although this huge, open-plan old pub has been given a typical brewery makeover – large restaurant area, wall bench seating, standard pub tables and chairs, and plates and prints on the walls, it is a convivial place to rest weary legs and, more importantly, it really welcomes families. You may be lucky enough to visit when hot-air balloons are taking off in the grounds.

about the pub

Hurt Arms
Ambergate, Belper
Derbyshire DE56 2EJ
Tel 01773 852006

DIRECTIONS: See Getting to the start
PARKING: 100
OPEN: daily, all day
FOOD: daily, all day Saturday and Sunday
BREWERY/COMPANY: Scottish Courage
REAL ALE: Marston's Pedigree, Timothy Taylor Landlord, Mansfield Bitter
DOGS: not allowed

Food

Expect to find an extensive menu listing traditional pub food. Meals are good value and portions very generous. Look to the 'steakhouse' menu for 16oz sirloin with all the trimmings, or opt for poached cod with cheese sauce, or one of the specials, perhaps lamb shank or pork steak in apple sauce.

Family facilities

There's an excellent children's play area (with a wood-chip base) to the rear of the lawned garden behind the pub – great for sunny days. If it's cold and rainy, then children are welcome inside away from the bar and there's a bargain kid's menu for them to peruse.

Alternative refreshment stops

The Black Swan by the Market Place in Crich or the Little Chef in Ambergate.

☛ Where to go from here

At the National Tramway Museum at Crich you can take a scenic journey through a period street to open countryside and travel on vintage trams from all over the world (www.tramway.co.uk).

The Five Pits Trail

CYCLE

Follow an undulating off-road route between former coal mines transformed into peaceful lakes and parks.

Former Coalfield

Sparse remnants of the Derbyshire section of the old Yorks, Notts and Derby Coalfield are now a delightful string of picnic areas, fisheries, country parks and nature reserves interlinked by the Five Pits Trail. Reclamation and conservation efforts over the past 30 years have seen spoil tips and wasteland replaced by rich hay meadows and maturing woodland, while the areas of water have attracted upwards of 200 species of birds. The former collieries had a long death, with deep mines gradually being replaced by huge opencast workings, which had a lifespan of less than 20 years.

Today's landscape holds only the barest scars of these workings, and these are slowly being disguised. The cornfields and pastures, meadows and woodland are probably the greenest this area has been for 150 years. Mining still plays its part, however. The fine bird reserves at Williamthorpe Ponds are partially filled by water pumped up from old workings from miles around. This is at a constant 10°C, and in winter attracts countless water birds to a frost- and ice-free home.

the ride

1 The **Tibshelf Ponds picnic site**, a popular place with locals and fishermen, is a picturesque mix of wooded glades, meadows and ponds where Tibshelf Colliery stood. The route is known as the Five Pits Trail, recalling busier days in this part of Derbyshire. Turn left from the car park, passing between ponds and up a short incline to a cross track. A **Five Pits Trail** board indicates the way back left, an initially rough path that soon meets a graded path, which you follow right. In a short distance you'll reach the rear of the **Wheatsheaf pub** and a descent beneath a road through an underpass. Rising again, turn right on to the compacted track. Crossing a rough lane, the way drops steeply down; don't speed, as the surface is badly rutted. This descent is matched by a long gradual climb and, soon, **Hardstoft Lane** picnic site.

2 Cross the road here, continuing along the firm track to reach **Locko Plantation**, planted in 1970, a mix of spruce, sweet chestnut and other strong growing species that clothe the remnants of the old spoil heaps at Pilsley Colliery. A very steep descent ends at a gate; carefully cross and pick up the trail opposite, rising again to cross **Timber Lane** into another picnic area. The track leaves left from the rear of this, rising gently to a junction. Here keep left, heading for **Grassmoor**. The next road crossing at the edge of **Williamthorpe** is rather busier, so take care here.

3 The next junction is at **Wolfie Pond**. Here, keep left for **Grassmoor** before forking right just before a gate. The open meadows here are typical of the reclaimed areas; more await you at **Grassmoor Country Park**, the end of the line. Spend time exploring the thickets, hay meadows and ponds before returning to an overbridge to commence the return journey.

4 A long, gradual climb returns you to **Wolfie Pond**, where you turn left for **Williamthorpe**. After a while pass through the outskirts of an industrial estate built on the site of another old colliery. A steep descent brings you to a wide bridge across a brook. Turn right along the wheelchair route, passing the large ponds before, at the far end, turning sharp left up an incline for **Holmewood**. Pause at the crossways at the top and look left to spot the distant, crooked spire of Chesterfield's parish church. Your way is right, soon reaching **Holmewood Bridge**. Dismount here, cross the bridge and rejoin the **Five Pits Trail** on the left, shortly crossing a busy road.

5 Pleasant woodland is superceded by cornfields and meadows before the outward route is rejoined at a junction. Follow signs for **Tibshelf** from here, crossing lanes with care.

6 Excellent views to the right (west) encompass the distant edge of the Peak District and the war memorial above **Crich**. Beyond the Wheatsheaf underpass, follow the trail back to **Tibshelf Ponds**, turning left at the lane to the car park.

Along the Five Pits Trail near Tibshelf

MAP: OS Explorer 269 Chesterfield & Alfreton

START/FINISH: Tibshelf Ponds picnic area, grid ref SK 441600

TRAILS/TRACKS: old railway and hard-surfaced tracks

LANDSCAPE: mixed immature woodland, hay meadows and cornfields, with views across Derbyshire to the Peak District

PUBLIC TOILETS: none on route

TOURIST INFORMATION: Chesterfield, tel 01246 345777

CYCLE HIRE: none near by

THE PUB: Weeping Ash Country Inn, Hardstoft, see Directions to pub, page 175

❶ Care to be taken at the road crossings. There are some short, steep climbs and some longer, gentler inclines

Getting to the start

From Chesterfield head south on the A61 through Clay Cross, turning on to the B6014 eastbound at Stretton (signed Tibshelf). At the edge of Tibshelf turn right on to the B6025, then very shortly left on the B6026 for Newton. In 300yds (274m) turn left into Shetland Road. In 500yds (457m) turn right into Sunny Bank. The car park is at the end of this road.

Why do this cycle ride?

This is a lovely ride along old railways and colliery tracks, long since reclaimed and now a green corridor between the resurgent pit villages of this part of Derbyshire. Excellent countryside and a fascinating heritage offer a moderately challenging route within sight of the edge of the Peak District.

Researched and written by: Neil Coates

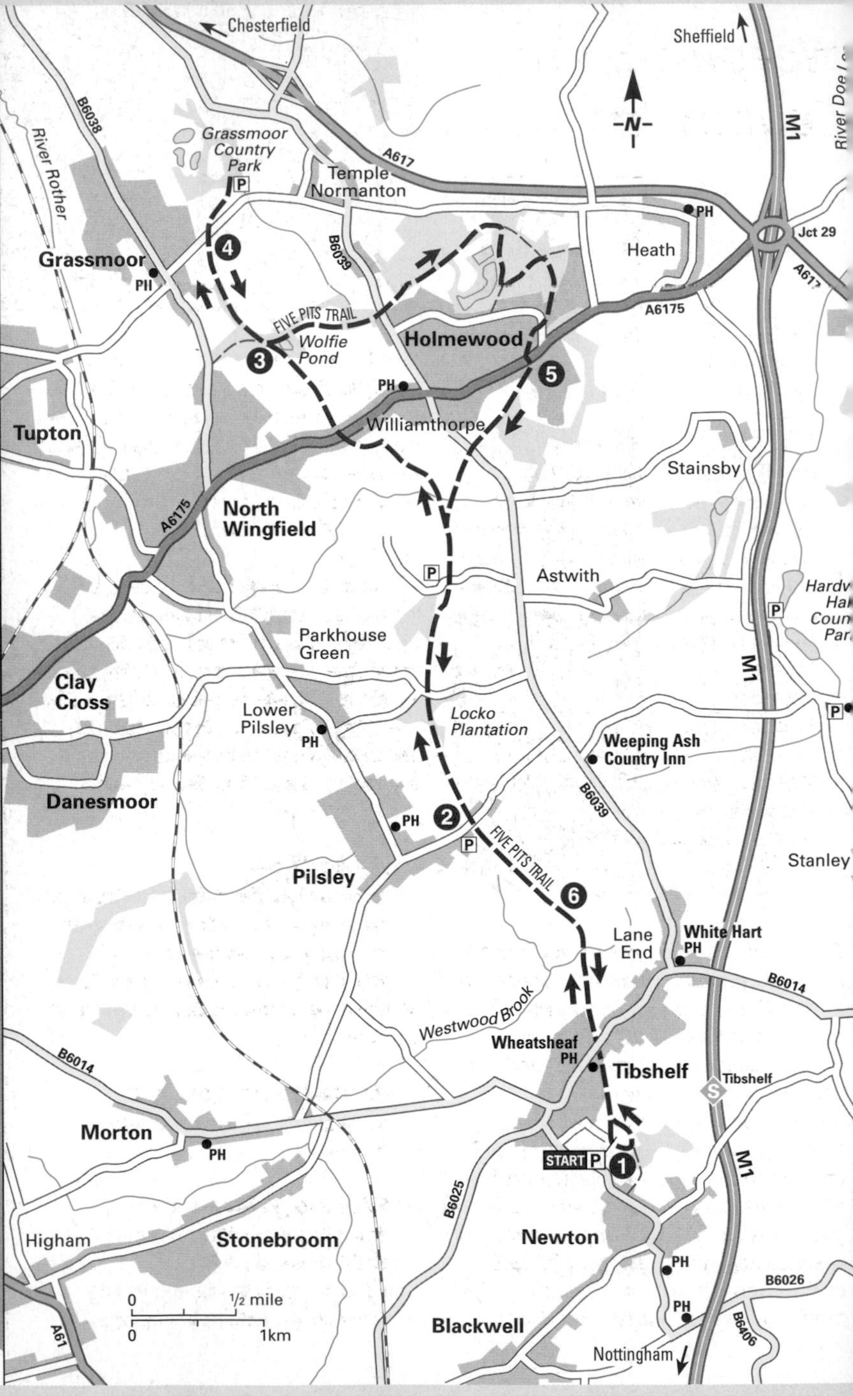

Five Pits Trail DERBYSHIRE

Chesterfield
Sheffield
River Dog
M1
B6038
River Rother
Grassmoor Country Park
A617
Temple Normanton
Heath
Jct 29
A617
④
Grassmoor
PH
PH
A6175
B6039
③
FIVE PITS TRAIL
Wolfie Pond
Holmewood
⑤
Tupton
PH
Williamthorpe
Stainsby
A6175
North Wingfield
P
Astwith
Hardwick Hall Country Park
Parkhouse Green
P
Clay Cross
Lower Pilsley
PH
Locko Plantation
Weeping Ash Country Inn
B6039
M1
P
Danesmoor
PH
②
Stanley
Pilsley
P
FIVE PITS TRAIL
⑥
Lane End
White Hart
PH
B6014
Westwood Brook
Wheatsheaf PH
Tibshelf
Tibshelf
S
B6014
Morton
PH
START P
①
M1
B6025
Newton
B6026
Higham
PH
½ mile
0
0
1km
Stonebroom
PH
Blackwell
Nottingham
A61

Weeping Ash Country Inn

about the pub

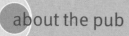

Weeping Ash Country Inn
Hardstoft, Chesterfield
Derbyshire S45 8AE
Tel 01246 850276

DIRECTIONS: from the Tibshelf Ponds car park return to the B6026 and the mini-roundabout accessing Tibshelf High Street. Turn right up the High Street and go through the village to a mini-roundabout at the White Hart pub. Turn left for Chesterfield (B6039) and drive for a mile (1.6km); the pub is on the right at a junction	
PARKING: 50	
OPEN: daily	
FOOD: no food Sunday evening	
BREWERY/COMPANY: free house	
REAL ALE: Hardys & Hansons Best, Old Trip, Mild, seasonal beers	
ROOMS: 7 bedrooms	

The Weeping Ash is a very comfortable and well-appointed country inn, catering for loyal local drinkers, a good passing trade and guests using the inn as a base for exploring this peaceful part of Derbyshire. As you would expect, weeping ash trees surround this rambling stone-built inn which stands in the heart of Hardstoft. Country sporting paraphernalia (gin traps, fishing rods, gun cases), local photographs, and a collection of porcelain adorn the walls and window sills within the comfortably furnished interior, which comprises a 'locals' bar, two lounge bars and two neatly laid-up dining areas. You'll find winter log fires, decent ale and a genuine warm welcome for walkers and cyclists. Bedrooms are housed in tastefully converted outbuildings.

Food
From a wide ranging bar menu, opt for the traditional chilli, liver and onions, bangers and mash or hot filled rolls or look to the specials board for something more imaginative, perhaps loin of venison with red wine and rosemary *jus* or pork loin on buttered mash with smoked bacon and cream sauce. There is a separate restaurant menu.

Family facilities
Children can let off steam in the play area by the car park and on fine days families can make good use of the small patio areas. Children are very welcome indoors where younger family members have their own menu.

Alternative refreshment stops
There are plenty of pubs and shops in Tibshelf.

☛ Where to go from here
Hardwick Hall, one of the most magnificent Elizabethan mansions in England, houses remarkable tapestries, furniture and woodwork (www.nationaltrust.org.uk).

Acknowledgements

The Automobile Association wishes to thank the following photo library and photographer for their assistance with the preparation of this book:

Photolibrary.com front cover b.
Neil Coates 17, 19, 20, 21, 23b, 24/5, 24b, 27, 29, 31t, 31b, 32, 35, 37, 39, 42, 47, 49, 53, 55, 57t, 59, 60, 64, 67, 79, 80, 83, 87t, 91, 95b, 99, 101t, 101b, 107, 111, 113, 115, 116/117, 119, 123t, 127, 129, 131, 132t, 132b, 135, 139, 141, 143, 144, 147t, 147b, 149, 151, 153b, 155, 159, 160, 163, 167, 168, 169, 171, 172, 173.

The remaining photographs are held in the Assocation's own photo library (AA World Travel Library) and were taken by the following photographers: .
Peter Baker 121, 153t; Jeff Beazley 85b, 87b; Malc Birkitt front cover ccr, 41, 73, 75, 105, 137; E A Bowness 12; Antony J Hopkins front cover cl, 4, 57b, 63b, 72, 85t, 89, 92/93, 93b, 95t, 109b, 123b, 125, 128, 136, 142, 145, 157, 165t, 166; Richard Ireland front cover cr, 23t, 43tr, 43tl, 50, 51, 63t, 69, 70, 71, 96, 103t, 103b, 104; Tom Mackie 15; Andrew Midgley 8/9, 77, 78, 109t, 165b; Tony Souter front cover ccl, 14b; Martin Trewlany 28; Wyn Voysey 13, 14t; Jonathan Welsh 44, 45.